My Struggle
with Faith

ALSO BY JOSEPH F. GIRZONE

Joshua

Joshua and the Children

Joshua in the Holy Land

Kara, the Lonely Falcon

The Shepherd

Never Alone

Joshua in the City

What Is God?

Joey

A Portrait of Jesus

Joshua: The Homecoming

Jesus, His Life and Teachings

The Parables of Joshua

The Messenger

Trinity

Joshua in a Troubled World

My Struggle
with Faith

Joseph F. Girzone

IMAGE BOOKS
DOUBLEDAY
New York London Toronto Sydney Auckland

AN IMAGE BOOK
PUBLISHED BY DOUBLEDAY

Copyright © 2006 by Joseph F. Girzone

All Rights Reserved

A hardcover edition of this book was originally published
in 2006 by Doubleday.

Published in the United States by Doubleday, an imprint of The Doubleday
Broadway Publishing Group, a division of Random House, Inc., New York.
www.doubleday.com

IMAGE, DOUBLEDAY, and the portrayal of a deer drinking from a stream are
registered trademarks of Random House, Inc.

Book design by Nicola Ferguson

Cataloging-in-Publication data is on file with the Library of Congress.

ISBN 978-0-385-51713-3

PRINTED IN THE UNITED STATES OF AMERICA

1 3 5 7 9 10 8 6 4 2

First Paperback Edition

DEDICATION

There have been individuals over the years since I began to write who have been an inspiration and support to me. Not only would I like to thank them for their continued interest and immense help, but I would like to dedicate this present work as a heartfelt thank-you to each of them. My dear friend and agent Peter Ginsberg tops that list. He has been a most loyal support through these many years. In difficult times, even when my faith in myself began to wane, he never lost faith in the messages we were sending out to the world. Trace Murphy, my editor ever since his arrival at Doubleday, has been most patient and helpful during the sometimes complicated birthing process of each of my books. His understanding and professional guidance have always been most encouraging. Trace's assistants, Joan Biddle and Darya Porat, have been helpful in many ways, especially in bringing so many important details to Trace's attention. Michelle Rapkin was the first publishing official to see value in *Joshua*, my first book to be published. She, with Peter Ginsberg's nudging, launched my writing career, and in her various capacities has been a support ever since. Bill Barry, publisher of Doubleday Religion, though always in the background in his various official capacities, has been a strong supporter of all my writings, especially at critical times. I am also grateful to Brad Broyles, my assistant and dear friend, for the great amount of help he has provided for so long a time, for his patient reading of my manuscripts, and for his professional suggestions. Richard and Elizabeth Della Ratta, besides being my legal advisors, have read all my manuscripts and made valuable suggestions before their transmission to the publisher. I am sure there are many others, especially the various artists and copy editors and other support persons at Doubleday, who have been critical in the publishing of my books. I am most grateful to all of them. And the one person who has been an essential part of the Joshua ministry for many years and still continues the mission is Sister Dorothy K. Ederer. She has raised it from the level of work to a most joyful adventure in spreading the Joshua messages far and wide.

CONTENTS

INTRODUCTION

So many people have asked me if my beliefs are the same as what Joshua expresses in the Joshua novels. Rather than answer each one as the question is put to me, since the answers are not simple and Joshua does not teach a complete compendium of Jesus' teachings, I have decided to explore with you what I believe. Belief itself is not simple. It is not a single conviction or idea. It is a complex network of convictions that subconsciously evolves over a lifetime into what becomes our philosophy of life, and the engine that drives us, and in the process transforms all our relationships with God and all God's creatures.

In this book I will try to explain my beliefs. This is not an easy task. My beliefs are very personal. My beliefs today are the end product of the long and complicated process that I endured—and I mean endured because the process was often painful. My search did not produce a set of infallible conclusions. Many others may not agree with the conclusions I arrived at in my long years of searching. I have tried to be honest with myself, and logical throughout the whole process, but being a frail human being, it is possible that I accepted wrong premises as the bases for evaluation of thoughts and beliefs, with the inevitably questionable conclusions that may have missed the target.

Developing a philosophy of life is not an easy process. It takes years of searching, of deep, critical thought, and the courage to embrace what you have found, especially when it prompts you to make decisions that may be different from where you have been all your life.

Some painful decisions that I had to make changed the course of my life. I was frightened about what the future might bring. I felt alone, terribly alone, and lonely. Only as I grew older did I see how those decisions opened up for me a whole new world, an exciting world of adventure that would never have happened had I not made those decisions.

In writing about this, I will also try to explain what the search has meant to me and what my beliefs have meant to me, especially in the later years of my life. I hope this expression of what I believe and why I believe what I believe will be a help to others who are struggling to develop their own understanding of life and in the process find a warm, intimate relationship with God and a renewed appreciation for the precious treasure that Jesus has won for us.

MY STRUGGLE
WITH FAITH

1

IS THERE A GOD?

WHEN I WAS A CHILD, God was very much a part of my life. My father talked about God as if God were part of our family or, more appropriately, we were part of God's family. My mother leaned over my crib when I was really small and prayed to God for me. Later she knelt at my bedside and taught me prayers. God was a very real, almost a tangible part of my life. The world of the spirit was as real as a parade on Armistice Day, or the parade of circus wagons just off the railroad cars and carrying the lions and tigers down the main street on their way to the fairgrounds. My guardian angel was always by my side, and I had no difficulty believing when I was almost run over by a car one day that my guardian angel had saved my life.

Was that real faith in God? Or was it like faith in Santa Claus? Whatever it was, it gave me strength to face many childhood difficulties. I felt without any doubt that God was very much a part of my life and was always there to guide me and give me strength. When I made my First Communion, I firmly believed that in some beautiful way Jesus became present in my soul, in a way much more intimate than God's presence in nature. I hardly ever missed daily Mass and Communion. It was so beautiful. I talked to Jesus as my best friend.

That kind of faith is, like much of childhood, almost a world of fantasy, so wonderful and comforting and so secure. Adolescence, however, abruptly changes so much of that beautiful world, as what we accepted as fact because our parents told us it was now becomes the object of doubt and sometimes disillusionment. We question all that we have been taught to believe, wondering whether it is something that we can accept and believe because we conclude that it is believable and not just because our parents have told us so. It is a most shattering experience if we take it seriously. My first problem was the guilt I felt in questioning what I had been taught. But then I began to realize that I was not being disloyal; I was just trying to understand. My next question was: Am I losing my faith? I knew that my faith was still strong, but I had a need to understand why I believed. And that did not mean that I was losing my faith. Questioning is part of the process of adolescence. It is a time of growing and understanding, a time when we take stock of our childhood beliefs and reconsider them in the light of our own emerging intelligence. This process is inherent in our nature and prompts us to evaluate what we have been taught as children and either make it our own or reject it as unacceptable or unbelievable.

One of the beliefs that is the first to be questioned centers around God, a God we cannot see, hear, or in any way perceive, as God never responds when we talk to Him. The first question that crosses an adolescent's mind is "How did my parents know about God? Who told them? Do I just believe what they told me about God because they are my parents? That is no reason to believe." But my crisis was not put into words like that. My crisis occurred after I had gone into the seminary at the age of fourteen. During my first year there I felt such peace. God was more intimate than ever, and I would spend time alone just thinking about God and feeling the wonderful closeness of a divine presence. That lasted for about a year. Then in my sophomore year it came to a devastating end.

I could no longer *feel* God's presence. I could no longer *feel* the love of Jesus in Communion. My heart had turned cold and empty. I became depressed and frightened. With whom could I share this agony, or who could even understand what I was going through? I felt so alone. We spent a lot of time in prayer in the seminary, and read scripture, and had beautiful talks about God and the spiritual life, but it all left me cold. The only experience that lifted my spirit was a daily class Father Gregory Smith taught about the life of Jesus. To hear him talk about Jesus made Jesus real and brought Him very close. But after the class the emptiness took over again. I could not pray. It was a drudge. It was without feeling or comfort.

Had I lost my faith? No, not really. I still sensed that underneath my parents' belief in God and the world of the spirit there had to be some solid evidence, but now I felt I had to find that evidence for myself. Saint Peter's counsel to the early Christian community, "Find a reason for your faith," became my mantra. My whole life, every waking moment, was a relentless pursuit of evidence for the reality of God. It was not always conscious, it was often subconscious. I began to see evidence of hidden influences in the many coincidences that took place in our lives, not just in my life but in the lives of other students and in the lives of the priests who taught us. Most of them were Irish priests who had seen and heard much about the Irish people's four hundred years of struggle to preserve their faith through brutal persecutions. Their rulers did all they could to annihilate them because they would not abandon their Catholic faith. Nothing seemed to be haphazard. The lives of these priests were an inspiration to me, and in a subtle way they hinted at the existence of a God protecting these people's faith through all those cruel centuries. It was not a direct proof for the reality of God, but it insinuated in me an attitude of trust in a being who cared enough to bring those people not through forty years in the desert of Sinai but through four hundred years of hardship and persecution under tyrants determined to destroy them.

Scripture study of the Exodus was another stunning example of outside influences on people's lives. The Exodus of the Hebrews from Egypt through a barren desert—which people seemed to accept as historically true—was a great support. A minimum of a quarter of a million people (many scholars estimate that number to be too low) were led by Moses to the Promised Land. The trip took forty years. Many died along the way; many were born along the way. What was the source of food for a quarter of a million people every day for forty years? Yet religious scholars do not doubt the authenticity of that monumental passage of a whole population. Moses attributed the success of the trip and even the steady supply of food to the benevolence of God. Evidence of God's existence? Not scientific evidence, but a powerful phenomenon to be considered. I accepted this whole story as historically true, though for centuries there was no evidence outside of scripture that those events ever took place. And many people did question the authenticity of the Exodus story, and cynics ridiculed the suggestion that God fed the Israelites miraculously for forty years. And I knew that I would not have wanted the responsibility of providing for a quarter of a million people every day, and for forty years. Even the thought depressed me.

These thoughts passed through my mind not as conclusive evidence but as suggestions of possibilities. My soul was still empty and obsessed with a frightful feeling of being alone. I had left my family, and I knew it was for good, and had chosen to live with a group of strangers. Some I liked; some I could never relate to. I felt like a pilgrim in a world of people so different from the way I was raised. I felt deprived of the comfort of the God who was always so much a part of my life.

At night I would slip down to the chapel and, in the darkness and emptiness, hope I would find God again. It didn't happen. I just sat there dumb and broken. Gradually a deep depression drifted through my being like a heavy fog that settles on a mountainside and obliterates all reality of the village below. The spirit world was now deeply lost in that fog, and all the joy and comfort it used to bring me.

I still clung to my calling to the priesthood. Deep down I knew I had to be where I was. I don't know why I knew it, whether it was destiny or a need to bring something important to people. My calling never wavered. I just knew, and that knowledge was like an anchor that held me secure, like an anchored vessel on a stormy sea. Nothing could shake me, not even the realization that I still had ten more years of study before my ordination. How could I endure it? What was the force that held me so tenaciously and would not let me waver or be shaken? Was it just a teenager's dogged determination? It could not have been that. The pull to go home and enjoy the companionship of girls was strong. Yet even that could not shake my resolve to follow what I felt was my destiny. Was "destiny" just another word for a divine plan? Was it God hiding beneath all the anguish? Something that happened frequently made me wonder even more about God's involvement in life. Insights about God, and flashes of understanding about people, even bad people, taught me to look on even the most contemptible as immortal beings with a personal destiny given to them by God and to recognize that even they had within them a goodness that God decided was necessary to touch some people's lives, people whom no one else could touch. It was therefore important for us to see these people not as the rejects of society but as children of God whose limited goodness was needed by God for a special purpose. I had many other flashes of awareness and insights into the nature of God, and our relationship with God, and the place of sinners in the plan of redemption. These and other lights emanating not from my own logical mind were beginning in a very subtle way to tell me that, even though I no longer had the *emotional* sense of God's presence, that presence was revealing itself in a much deeper way and at a higher level than mere emotion, as if God was leading me somewhere that was unfamiliar, communicating with me, sharing with me His own understanding of life and of so many things that were powerfully shaping my thinking.

When someone talks to you, you know they are talking to you. When these flashes of light came to me, I knew someone was communicating messages to me. I did not know who, but I knew the messages were not mine. One insight in particular was shocking. I had always felt that capital punishment was theologically justified because it was allowed and prescribed in the Old Testament. But this new insight told me that when people execute someone, they are tearing that person out of God's hands and refusing to allow God to continue His unfinished work in that soul. The thought frightened me; I began to see capital punishment as more evil than murder, because it was the act of the self-righteous intentionally snatching from the Creator a person whom God was still in the process of saving. From then on I saw execution as an arrogant assault on God's control over human life and as a subtle denial of belief in God. I could see clearly then that the executioner and those demanding execution are no different in God's eyes from the murderer who tries to justify his crime. Both deny to the Creator control over human life, the right to finish the divine work of redemption in the souls of those they execute.

Another issue I grappled with was God's ability to know what goes on in the life of every single human being and in each part of this vast creation. One night, in a brief flash of awareness for which I could take no credit, a most beautiful thought crossed my mind. The experience lasted for not more than one second. God's presence is throughout all creation. When the sun rises in the morning, its rays touch everything in creation at the exact same instant. If God's mind is like the sun's rays, then God knows all the intimate details of all our lives in a single instant. From that day on I could see clearly how God could be everywhere and also continuously aware of every detail of our lives, and of every happening in the universe, in one moment of time.

Biology class was for me a gold mine of ideas. Studying the structure of the human eye, with all the complex components of highly specialized tissues and nerve cells and fluids, all coming together perfectly synchronized in the fully developed eye, was so impressive it made me wonder. Did this happen as the final product of a haphazard evolution? And did that process also include the independent development of the human ear, with all its complex parts, especially the cochlea, with its twenty thousand specially designed hairlike nerve cells, each one sensitive to a certain wave frequency, which gives us the ability to distinguish such a wide variety of sounds and combinations of sounds? And all this is perfectly synchronized with what the eye is seeing at any particular time, so there is not the slightest lapse of time before the ear hears what the eye sees.

Some would have us believe that this marvelous phenomenon was the product of an evolution haphazardly driven by the natural need of living organisms. For me to accept that would have taken more faith than to believe that there was some kind of intelligence behind the complex working of creation. It was still not exactly real scientific evidence of the existence of God, but it was a powerfully persuasive suggestion of the possibility of the existence of some kind of intelligent force manipulating nature into producing highly complex organisms and organs capable of working together in an intelligent and highly efficient fashion, and even more remarkably, with the ability to reproduce themselves. Some insist that these phenomena occurred as the need surfaced. By chance? By accident? To insist that I believe that, I felt, was an assault on my intelligence.

But the next question that came to my mind was about the existence of the world and the whole universe. Was it just always here and in need of no explanation, or was it created by an intelligent force? If it was always here, then it must be responsible for its own existence, and must have all the intelligent forces of chemical, magnetic, electrical, and gravitational powers automatically present within itself from all eternity, a god unto itself, which gave rise to all the complex forms of life on earth today. That idea troubled me because everything in this universe seems to function intelligently, and mere dirt or primal gases cannot possibly have intrinsic intelligence. This all led me to the conclusion that the universe cannot be responsible for its own existence, which would have to be the case if there was nothing outside itself. What would further follow from that is that the universe would have to be holding itself in existence at each moment and at each moment be responsible for the continuity of its processes. That seemed an impossibility.

The only other option was an intelligent force that created the universe and was responsible for all the laws governing the movements and evolution of this vast creation.

The problem then was: From where did this intelligent force come? When did it begin? Did it have a beginning? Could it be eternal? What could explain in an intelligent way its eternal existence? No answer to that even seemed possible, but the existence of the universe is a fact, a very tangible fact. That it could not be the answer to its own merely material nature made sense. So, the only possible explanation had to be an intelligent force, an intelligent being outside of nature that created everything. How this being began is a question human intelligence could never answer, but since there is a creation that is very real to us, the existence of this being has to be a reality as well, even though we cannot explain its origin.

That question settled, though not scientifically proven, I passed on to the next issue. Since intelligent beings also have the ability to make decisions, this intelligent being has to have willpower, a power that is of necessity omnipotent. Though there is no way to be absolutely certain about the eternal existence of this being, I was faced with the existence of a very concrete world all around me that had to have some explanation outside itself. That meant that a previously existing intelligent being had to have the power to will other beings into existence. It had to have the ability to create. It also had to have the ability to love, since creation is an expression of love.

Now, this entire energy-draining search was not done in a short time. The process obsessed me for many years. Even on my ordination day I could still not feel there was a God. I believed more than ever that God was real, but it was a belief that went much deeper than an emotion. I had become acutely aware that God was communicating with me at a deeper level. It was not as emotionally comforting or satisfying as feeling God's presence, but it was enlightening and satisfying intellectually.

The question that logically came to mind was: Just because I am convinced there is an intelligent presence communicating with me, how can I be sure it is God? Could it be my subconscious or something inside me? At the time, I had been reading the writings of Edith Stein, the German-Jewish phenomenologist, who studied under Edmund Husserl in the late 1930s. Phenomenology taught that what we experience through our senses and through our intelligence is not fantasy but reality. Edith Stein had been an atheist. One weekend she visited friends. During her stay she spent a whole night in their library reading the autobiography of Saint Teresa of Avila and the recounting of her mystical experiences of God. Convinced of the down-to-earth, commonsense personality of the saint, Edith concluded that Teresa had really experienced God in some way. For a phenomenologist, that was a powerful reason to accept the existence of God. So, when she finished the book early the next morning, she remarked, "This is the truth. There is a God." And she purchased a catechism and other books to prepare for her conversion.

The conclusion of this brilliant woman, who was one of the greatest philosophers in Germany at that time, made a deep impression on me and helped me realize the validity of my own experiences of God.

2

CREATION OF THE UNIVERSE

*h*OW THE UNIVERSE CAME about was a simple problem after the question of God's existence was resolved, even if it was not totally answered from a purely scientific standpoint. But then, even though some scientists reject the existence of God because there is no scientific evidence of His existence, they still accept many other things on faith. Otherwise they would never read newspapers or scientific journals. They have to accept on faith what they read.

The existence of the universe presented many problems. The first was whether it could coexist with God but separate from God. There was no point in even wasting time to consider whether the universe existed alongside the eternal existence of God. It was an easily accepted conclusion that if there was a God, the universe was a creation of God's genius.

What was of interest, however, was the manner in which

God created the universe. The Book of Genesis seems to indicate that God created everything over a period of time—six days, if Genesis is scientifically correct. But that did not seem to make sense. First of all, it says God created light first, then almost as an afterthought, two days later, created the sun and the moon, and then the other lights of the heavens. According to Genesis, the earth was flat, and there was half a globe covering the earth, with the lights from heaven hanging like so many chandeliers. Even as a child, I had never felt the Genesis account of creation was a historical record. It seemed too much like a story an adult would tell children to teach a lesson. It was poetic, and had the hallmark of a fable or a fairy tale. The kernel of truth was its essence. There was a God, the only God, who created this whole vast universe and everything in it. There was not a sun god as in Egypt, and a god of fertility, and more gods to satisfy other human needs. There was only one God, who created all things. That was an undeniable truth that I had no trouble believing.

Did this God create every living thing on different days, as described in Genesis? That presented a problem for me. The question immediately comes to mind: What does a "day" mean? Does God follow a calendar? Are there days in eternity? What meaning would a "day" have to God? Did this Creator will everything into existence all at once, or were creatures scheduled into existence? Did God create each species of plant and animal? Why are there no more dinosaurs, or animals closely related to dinosaurs, or tall, forty-foot fern trees like those existing three or four hundred million years ago?

One day I encountered a fundamentalist Christian. In discussing creation, he said that, according to the Bible, the universe is only six thousand years old. I said that that could not be. Fossils have been proven to be hundreds of millions of years old. His response was that it may seem that way, but God actually created fossils. I could not resist countering that if God did that, then God is lying, attempting to deceive us, and that cannot be. The fossils have to be the age that scientists calculate. We have to accept truth wherever we find it. It did not seem that God created in the manner described in Genesis. There is so much change in nature, so much ongoing change, even today, that just keen observation strongly suggests that the Creator instituted a dynamic process that was to unfold over millions, even billions of years. It seemed to me to be a fitting way for God to create.

You see change continually taking place in the inanimate world. The landmass of the earth has shifted dramatically over many thousands of years. There existed vast forests of fern trees and plants hundreds of millions of years ago. When I was stationed in Pottsville, Pennsylvania, many years ago, there was a huge hill of dumpings from the coal mines just behind the monastery. I would take walks through those hills and pick up chunks of coal, some containing two-foot-wide fossils of fern trees and large slabs of fossils of fern fronds. Nowhere on earth do these trees exist today, except in the form of small ferns growing along our forest floors.

Those gigantic fern trees lived in the times of the dinosaurs, which we no longer have today except in the form of some amphibians or lizards that resemble dinosaurs but are minute by comparison. Could they be related? It would seem so, as their characteristics are so strikingly similar.

In biology class I was introduced to evolution, but only as

a hypothesis, not an accepted fact. I was fascinated by it and read all I could get my hands on. I talked with professors and colleagues and went to conventions later on when I was teaching biology. I met a biologist who taught at a Jewish high school. He told me he had been talking to a science teacher from an evangelical school who told him the world was six thousand years old. He asked if I as a Catholic believed that. I said no. When he asked me how I felt about God, religion, and science, I told him I did not have a problem with it. He was surprised. I told him I believed that God is the Creator of nature and the Author of the Bible. God cannot contradict in revelation what He has placed in nature. The biologist thought that made a lot of sense, and was going to bring that back to his students.

I, however, had a lot of problems with the concept of evolution. I could see the many similarities among members of various species of animals, and plants as well. Similarities in the development of organs in the embryos of animals of different species were stunning. The genealogy of modern horse from ancient eohippus is overwhelming in the wealth of evidence presented for its evolution from simpler forms. The development of amphibians is also impressive, but in all the apparent chains of evidence attempting to explain the development of various species, there seemed to be too many gaps that had to be bridged before I could be convinced that that chain of events reflected what actually took place. Scientists believe that necessity gave rise to development of new organs over millions of years. How could anyone prove that? It seemed a purely gratuitous supposition. While I was studying at Columbia University, our laboratory was next to Professor

Morgan's old laboratory. Professor Morgan's claim to fame was his experiments with fruit flies. During those years of experimentation, his students oversaw more generations of fruit flies than there were generations of human beings since our beginning. They exposed those fruit flies to every possible type of environment and condition including various chemical treatments and radiation. At the end of all these experiments, the fruit flies were hardly different from the original pair they started out with. That set me back in trying to be open to evolution. But I still felt that there had to be evolution of some kind, as there were too many similarities between plants of different species and animals of different species.

However, as far as my religious convictions were concerned, it made no difference whether evolution was a fact or whether God created individual species. I always thought that if God began His creation as a submicroscopic spool of genetic matter and endowed it with the ability to unfold gradually over millions of years, it would be a beautiful way for Him to create. To say that God created individual species of plants and animals at various times seemed to portray Him as a child playing in a sandbox and creating plants and animals at random. It attributed to the Creator a capricious manner of bringing beings into existence. That would be so different from the orderly unfolding of the rest of the universe that it did not make sense to me.

Thinking through the problems of creation and its beginning helped to settle my mind. It also helped me see the *necessity* for an intelligent and all-powerful God; but necessity for the existence of something is still not scientific proof of its existence, even though it is a small step away from that conclusion. As far as the mind is concerned, psychologically it can feel satisfied that God exists even though the technical evidence is not conclusive and points only to the *necessity* of God's existence. If I can see shadows falling from the trees in my backyard, I may not see the sun, but I can feel certain the sun is shining. It may not be proof, but it is powerful evidence nonetheless. No one has ever seen an atom, but the shadows cast from an atom in an electron microscope are strong enough evidence for scientists to *believe* that atoms exist. Everything I read in a scientific journal I accept on faith that the scientist who wrote a particular article based on his own original research has accurately performed the work he is expounding and is honest in his presentation of the evidence.

This struggle with God and my faith lasted for years. Deep down I believed, but I had to find a reason why I believed. We all do. Saint Peter's counsel "Find a reason for your faith" stayed with me all my life, not just in matters of religion but even in those of less importance.

I will never forget the moment I was being ordained. I was lying prostrate on the marble floor in the sanctuary of the cathedral while the bishop prayed over us. I explained the scene during a retreat years later and said very trustingly that deep down I believed in God, though I still could not *feel* there was a God. A few weeks later I read in a radical conservative national Catholic newspaper that "Girzone admitted that on the day of his ordination, he did not believe in God." That was the first time in my life I came across character assassination on the part of religious people. Obviously there was a spy at the retreat who reported me, and the editor never had the decency to ask if what he was printing was what I had actually said. This was so different from my experience with a secular magazine. *People* magazine did an article on me. Their research person called me at least four times before the article was published to ask if I was being quoted accurately. One would think that the publisher of a religious newspaper would be even more concerned about truth and, even more, about a priest's reputation. Perhaps the chance to destroy a priest's character was more enticing than concern for truth.

Finding a reason for faith became a mantra. As I grow older I understand more and more the wisdom of Saint Peter's counsel. I now live on a mountainside. When I look out the window and can see across to three states, this thought never fails to cross my mind: The world is so real and so beautifully awesome in its order and obedience to the laws that control it, it certainly cannot have created and programmed itself. A person may ask, "Well, if you feel a God has to have created the world, then where did God come from? Who created God?" I think there are only two possible answers: Either the universe is God, or an eternally existing intelligent being is God, the God whose intelligence is reflected in the orderliness of an unintelligent mass of matter that issued from God's creative power. It takes less faith to believe in an eternal intelligent God than to believe in a mass of matter that has no consciousness. So, my own mantra is reduced to a simple observation. I know there is a God, because the world exists, and I know it is real, and not an illusion, because I perceive it with my senses and I can analyze it with my intelligence, which I also am conscious exists.

As we grow older and reflect on the many personal incidents that occur in our lives, we cannot help but sense that there is someone prompting us to do something, and when this happens frequently, it would seem foolish to even think it could be just a coincidence or a series of coincidences. One particular incident is a good example. Since my retirement, I rarely wear my Roman collar or black suit. One day, as I was leaving my parents' house, I had the strongest urge to wear my black suit and Roman collar. I did not know why, but I went back into the house and changed.

As I was driving over a bridge spanning the Hudson River, I saw a group of police cars with flashing lights at a place where the road splits. Sensing that something dramatic was taking place, I stopped and asked a policeman what had happened.

"That young man standing on that railing over there is threatening to jump into the river. When we try to approach him, he tells us to stay back or he will jump. We don't know what to do."

"Do you mind if I try to talk to him?" I asked.

"Not at all. We can't do anything. You might as well try."

I walked away from the police and stayed at a distance from where the young man was perched on the bridge railing, holding on to a post.

"Can I help you, young fellow?" I called out to him.

Turning around, he looked over, saw me dressed in my priest's garb, and relaxed.

"Hi, Father!" he responded.

"What happened?"

He then poured his heart out to me as I slowly walked closer.

"Would you like to come with me over to the coffee shop around the corner and tell me all about it?"

"Yeah, I'd like that, Father, because I'm all confused."

I helped him down, and we walked to my car. We both got in, and as I was driving off, I stopped momentarily next to a policeman and told him where we were going, and told him to have one of the cars follow and wait outside until we were finished talking. I knew they would insist he go to the psychiatric center. I said we would follow them to the center. It all turned out well. The boy's mother called later after reading about the incident in the evening paper. She was so happy that her son came home alive.

After the incident, I went back home and sat down at the kitchen table and told my mother what had happened. So many things like that happen that it must be more than just coincidence, especially when people's lives are concerned. One day I had the strongest urge to visit somebody. I had just finished offering Mass and was on my way to breakfast. I struggled with the thought of going to see this person and tried to cast it off so I could have my breakfast. However, something told me I had to go and visit that man immediately, so I did. When I got there, I arrived just in the nick of time, as he was about to plunge a butcher knife into his stomach. After much counseling, his whole depressed life changed, and he entered a profession where he has been able to work at healing many others.

On another occasion, close to midnight, I was getting ready for bed. I was totally drained after a hard day's work. Something, however, told me to go to the hospital and visit a person who had brain cancer and was not expected to live. Again, I struggled against it, but finally gave in and went to the hospital. The man was surprised to see me at such a late hour, but appreciative nonetheless. I talked to him for a few minutes, since I really wanted to get home and go to bed. Before leaving, I prayed and asked God's blessing upon him, and gave him the sacrament of the sick. A few days later he came home from the hospital totally healed. Scientific proof? No. But I would have to be dense to deny that I was being moved by someone outside me.

3

ART REFLECTING THE
SOUL OF THE ARTIST

AFTER I FELT RELATIVELY COMFORTABLE with my new and more intellectual foundation for belief in God as Creator of the universe, this universe then took on a different image. It now became for me a massive sculpture, a masterpiece of scientific art. I will never forget an experience I had with a master artist when I was a young priest. The artist's name was John Trost. A recent convert who previously had been the editor of a Communist newspaper in Paris during the Great War, John was referred to me by the founder of the Edith Stein Guild, Leon Paul. As I came to know John and learned more about his background as an artist, I asked if he would scan some artworks by a young high school student. The student's teacher asked if I would view them and comment on them. There were perhaps fourteen four-foot-square oil paintings. Thinking John would provide a much better evaluation of the paintings, I showed them to him.

He looked at each one for no more than ten seconds, then turned to the next one. His review took him little more than a minute. When I asked him what he thought, he immediately replied, the student is a boy about fourteen years old, and Jewish, as was John, and the boy had considerable talent. His work, however, showed that he was a deeply troubled boy.

I was amazed that he could see so much in a quick glance at a work of art, but it told me a lot—a message I never forget—that the soul of an artist is reflected in his or her paintings.

If the universe is the artwork of God, it must tell us much about what kind of a "soul" God has and what this creation reflects of God's inner life.

I spent many hours trying to understand God from observing nature and humans' sensitivity to it. One of my first observations was the colors in nature and our ability to perceive them. The universe could have been designed in black and white. On dreary, black-and-white days, we feel depressed. Places where there is little sunshine and long dreary rainy spells occasion more frequent incidents of severe depression. Even the birds respond to bright, sunny days. The trees outside my bedroom are alive with birdsong at sunrise on those days. On dark mornings there is no happy birdsong.

Fortunately, nature is in living color, with the shades of color changing all day long. Not many people take time to notice, but these thousands of different colors and shades of color play a very important role in our emotional and psychological health. We respond very strongly to the colors in nature. Again, we are most fortunate that they are soft and gentle. The sky is delicate blue, not heavy purple. The clouds are for the most part soft, feathery silver or fluffy white. Dark clouds are frightening and ominous. Horror movies paint dark, stormy clouds in the background of scenes to heighten the drama of impending evil. Trees that fill most of the earth are soft green, and in the fall they turn to quiet, pastel colors. Joshua house, where I live, is framed every fall in a glorious display of pastel red, orange, yellow, and purple foliage of a thousand shades. When the leaves fall from the trees and the forests are bare, and the cold, wintry days set in, so does the gloom. We long for the few sunny days of winter and the magic of a new-fallen snow to brighten our days. We bring color into our homes at Halloween and Thanksgiving and Christmas, since there is no color outside. We crave color. It is exciting and exhilarating.

What does this say about the Artist who designed nature? It says a lot. Our life on this earth is not intended to be a prison or a punishing experience. It is intended to be a joyful experience, filled with song and laughter and happy relationships. When the birds sing in the morning, they sing not just for themselves but to send out messages to all their friends. When nature is alive with bright color, we come alive and want to share our joy and gather for picnics, and boating, and have good times with friends. When it is dismal, we hide, like the birds. It is hard to find them on dark days unless you have a bird feeder.

Another observation is the unimaginable combinations of flavors available in all the foods spread out before us and the ability of our sense of taste to discern these flavors, judging whether they are good or bad, pleasant or distasteful, then to enjoy the ones we like. If we take the time to focus, we can become almost ecstatic over a favorite entrée, a special dessert, or a perfect cordial. Isn't it interesting that we can pick grapes and they turn into a delicious wine that cheers the heart, as it says in the Bible? What does that say about God? He is a God full of fun who wants to spread happiness through pleasure and joy. It is hard to imagine these natural phenomena to be products of a series of accidents. It takes too much faith to believe that. We also find in nature herbs and naturally manufactured chemicals that can cure hundreds of human illnesses.

And then there are the objects designed and manufactured by human genius, many made with uncanny precision of the most complex and refined physical substances and put together to perform the most delicate of tasks, some even imitating human intelligence, as in computers. Then consider that all these incredibly beautiful and complex creations of divine and human genius are made basically of nothing more than common dirt. When we sit back and think of the crass building blocks of our world, it is not difficult to imagine that the world where God dwells is much more beautiful and refined than our own. Perhaps God designed this world to give us hints of a world where spiritual beings like Him live. If so, is that a world that we might one day see?

If art reflects the soul of the artist, then the universe provides us with endless insight into the mind and heart of God.

4

DOES GOD REALLY CARE?

*I*T IS SAID THAT ARISTOTLE, the ancient Greek philosopher and one of the greatest thinkers ever, arrived at the realization that there is a God who created and ruled the world. But for years Aristotle struggled with the question as to whether God cared for His human creatures. As brilliant as Aristotle was, he felt a gnawing need for intimacy with God. He sensed and craved what many centuries later Saint Augustine so beautifully expressed when he wrote, "Our hearts were made for you, O God, and they will only rest when they rest in you." Aristotle never found what Augustine found, intimacy with God and the realization that God cared. One day Aristotle's body was found on the shore of a lake—some think, the victim of suicide. There is a need in the human soul for intimacy with a being outside us, a being we sense is greater than ourselves, who can give depth of meaning to our existence. We are not comfortable with the feeling we are just animals, even if a more highly developed variety. We instinctively sense there is something more to us than just an animal nature. These are the questions I want to discuss in this chapter: Does God really care? Are we in any way special to God, more so than the rest of the animal creation? Can we have an intimate relationship with God?

The answers to these questions cannot come from reason or any kind of deductive thinking. The answers have to come from verifiable human historical experience. We can ask: Did God ever manifest in a concrete, tangible way that He had any real personal interest in His human creatures?

The Bible presents a possible help in answering this question, but we have to approach the Bible not as a book of spiritual truths but as an account of verifiable historical events that took place in the life of a very special people in an age long past. So, it is the Hebrew Bible, or the Old Testament, that is important to us in this search.

The Hebrew Bible recounts events in the life of the descendants of a man called Abram. Abram was, according to the Bible, a very special person. He originally lived in Chaldea, which is modern Iraq. A messenger was supposedly sent to him by God to tell him to leave his people and his country and follow wherever God led him, which the Bible records he did.

According to the Bible, God changed Abram's name to Abraham. Abraham had two sons, Isaac and Ismail. Isaac was the son by his wife; Ismail was by his wife's slave. In time Isaac married and had two sons, Jacob and Esau. Jacob married and had twelve sons, who eventually grew into the twelve tribes of Jacob, more commonly referred to as the twelve tribes of Israel, the name-change God gave to Jacob. During a famine throughout the whole region, Jacob and his extended family migrated to Egypt at the invitation of Jacob's son Joseph, who had been sold by his jealous brothers as a slave and in time ended up being Pharaoh's vizier for all Egypt.

As time passed, the children of Israel became slaves in Egypt, but ultimately, after enduring the harshness of slavery for 450 years, they were rescued by the miraculous intervention of Yahweh, the God who identified Himself to Moses. Moses was an Israelite who had been raised in Pharaoh's court, but through unfortunate circumstances fled Egypt and wandered through the desert in southern Arabia, where he married the daughter of a Midian herdsman. After many years Yahweh told Moses to go back to Egypt and tell Pharaoh to let God's people leave the country. Pharaoh refused, and God punished the Egyptians severely until Pharaoh finally relented.

After the Israelites left, Pharaoh changed his mind and sent his army to destroy the Israelites. The Israelites were well on their way, having crossed over into Sinai. Warned by God that Pharaoh's army was pursuing them, they traveled into the mountains toward Saudi Arabia; then they arrived at a beach on the Red Sea, in the Gulf of Aqaba, about seventy miles north of the mouth of the gulf. Recently this area has been the subject of intensive research. The biblical account says that God told Moses to strike the water with his staff. As soon as he struck the water, it parted and formed a dry pathway for the Israelites to escape to the other side. When Pharaoh's chariots tried to pass through, however, the waters closed and his army was destroyed.

After that episode, the Israelites under Moses' leadership wandered for forty years through the desert until God finally brought them to the land He had promised to Abraham centuries before. This whole story is accepted solely on what is written in a holy book. Did those events really happen, or is it just a story, like the Book of Mormon, which has no historical evidence to substantiate what is written? Did God really guide those people, and for all those years? The number of Israelites has been estimated variously as from 250,000 up to 1,200,000. That is a lot of people to feed and care for every day for forty years in a barren desert. They had little food other than what they took with them. Even if they took cattle and sheep, how long would even a huge herd last feeding such a huge number of people? And for long periods of time there was no water available.

How did they eat? How could they survive for all those years? Is the story fictitious, or an exaggeration of a real historical event? Or could it have happened as the Bible records, with God caring for them all that time? The answers to those questions were critical to me because they would tell me whether there is evidence of God really caring for His human creatures. If there is evidence from archeology or from secular writings of the same time that corroborates the story of Moses and the Israelites fleeing Egypt and wandering through the desert for forty years, then I could have a basis to believe that God really had shown concern for His human creatures.

Until recently there was little evidence that the children of

Abraham were ever in Egypt, and even less evidence that they spent forty years wandering through the desert. It is only in the last thirty years that archeologists and historians have been uncovering significant amounts of evidence that the Hebrew people—the Apirus, as they were called in official Egyptian records of the time—did live in Egypt and that they left there in a great exodus around 1450 B.C.

There is also strong evidence that Israelites lived in the land of Goshen from around 1500 B.C. Archeologists discovered the remains of a village in the northern part of Egypt at Goshen. The materials found were not Egyptian but Asiatic in origin. The construction of the buildings was the same as that found centuries later in Israel, when the Israelites settled in the land of Canaan.

Concerning the Exodus, it was commonly believed that the Israelites crossed the Red Sea where the Suez Canal is located. After years of research, nothing was ever found to support that belief. Recently archeologists decided to follow the directions provided in the Book of Exodus itself and see where they would lead. Surprisingly, they led not to any place in the Sinai but to the Gulf of Aqaba and, even more surprisingly, to Arabia. The Bible talks about a large gorge between high cliffs. This description fit perfectly a beach seventy miles north of the mouth of the Gulf of Aqaba. That was the only place in the gulf (which the Bible called the Red Sea) where there was a gorge between high cliffs. A Swedish scientist, Lennart Möller, spent years researching the area and found remarkable evidence supporting the Exodus account in the Bible. He and another Swedish researcher, Viveka Ponten, discovered the wheels and axles of chariots scattered haphazardly on the floor of the sea and also, by itself, the remains of a chariot wheel with four spokes covered with electra, a combination of gold and silver. Four-spoke chariot wheels were unique to Egypt during the Eighteenth Dynasty, at the time of the Exodus, as shown in drawings from that period.

The researchers also discovered that the water is over five thousand feet deep there, but beginning at the beach on the west side of the gulf and ending at Arabia on the east side, there is a ridge near the surface, wide enough and solid enough for a large number of people to cross over. And that is exactly where the remains of the chariots were found.

According to villagers living in Saudi Arabia, long-standing traditions say that Moses was there at one time. There are still wells and other sites named after him.

Finally, there exists correspondence dating back to 1540 B.C. from the Canaanites complaining to Pharaoh of an invasion of people from the desert, overwhelming their land and destroying order. Canaan was still under Egyptian control during that time. At the same time that the Israelites were entering the Promised Land, the Canaanites were pleading for help to restore order to their country.

Knowing these facts made it possible for me to accept the reality of the Israelites wandering through the desert for all that time. The question that haunted me was: Who fed them for the forty years? Where would there be in a desert sufficient food and water to feed such a vast horde? The Bible says that they were fed by God. It is the only way they could have survived. I could accept the biblical account then as relatively honest, even though many accounts are exaggerated and contain a primitive people's interpretation of natural events, such as plagues and pestilence, as punishments from God.

The phenomenon of the Exodus alone was for me impressive evidence that God did care for His human creatures. That was a big step in my faith journey. I was slowly, painstakingly, finding a reason for my faith.

5

THE BIBLE:
HISTORY OR MYTH?

*t*HE BIBLE HAS ALWAYS BEEN looked on by Christians and Jews as inspired by God. What does that mean? Does it mean that everything in the Bible is inspired? Many good people in our own day and in days long past considered every word of the Bible to be inspired. Origen, an early Father of the Church and the most voluminous writer in history, with over six thousand volumes to his credit, believed early in his life not only that the Bible was inspired but that its literal meaning was inspired. As a result, when he read the following passage—"If your eye scandalizes you, pluck it out. It is better that you go into the other world with one eye than that you go to hell with both eyes; and if your hand scandalizes you, cut it off. It is better for you to go into heaven with one hand, than to go to hell with both hands"—Origen took those words of Jesus to heart, and even extended their meaning. Since he had a problem with chastity, he castrated himself. Only later, when he realized that Jesus was speaking figuratively to dramatize the importance of making sacrifices to maintain a virtuous life, did Origen regret what he had done.

Although many authors believed in a spiritual interpretation of the Bible, and others in allegorical interpretation, the literal interpretation was always considered sacred. The attachment to the literal interpretation of scripture has occasioned much religious strife through the centuries. Religious leaders and theologians were prone to take what scripture said about nature as scientifically accurate. When scientists tried to show that that was not possible, frightful scenes ensued and untold damage was done to people's faith in religion. The showdown with Galileo was over a similar issue. The Bible states that the sun stood still so the Israelites could successfully complete a battle with the opposing army. In the sixteenth and seventeenth centuries, Copernicus and Galileo had overwhelming data showing that the sun could not have stood still, because the sun does not move in its relationship with the earth. It is the earth that moves. Copernicus was the first to teach this, many years before Galileo, and he wrote about it without upsetting Church authorities. Many enlightened monks who were astronomers also accepted the evidence. When Galileo, with his testy, confrontational personality, came up with the same evidence and started circulating it widely, thus creating doubts in people's minds about scripture, he antagonized the very ones who were his supporters and were assigned to evaluate his work. Unlike Copernicus, Galileo was censured for disseminating ideas contrary to what is stated in the Bible. He was sentenced to house arrest in the palace of an archbishop who was a close friend. Not really a horrible punishment, but at the same time a censure by Church officials.

Even today with all our enlightenment, there is still no resolution of the problem of what is inspired in the Bible and whether God inspired each word, intending it to be taken literally. Furthermore, it is obvious that even people who believe in the literal interpretation do not really practice it in real life; otherwise there probably would be many one-eyed, one-handed men with high-pitched voices.

The problem is still a serious one. The first question that should be asked is: Who said the Bible is inspired?

It is not ordinary people who can make the decision. If ordinary people made the decision, others would not have an obligation to accept it and be required to base their faith and their lives on it. The decision has to be made by persons with authority for believers to be obliged to accept it as their way of life.

In the time of the ancient Israelites, there was such an authority, the authority established by Yahweh Himself. That authority was Moses, and he shared it with Aaron, the high priest. That teaching authority, or magisterium, as it is called, was passed on to the scribes, Pharisees, and high priests. Jesus recognized that teaching authority when He told His followers, "Do what the scribes and Pharisees tell you. They occupy the chair of Moses [their authority comes from God]. But do not imitate them because they are hypocrites."

It was this teaching authority in Judaism which declared for the Israelites that their scriptures were inspired by God. So, we see Jesus and the apostles using quotations from the

Old Testament as words coming from the mouth of God. Saint Paul testified to this when he wrote in his Second Letter to Timothy that "all scripture is inspired," referring to the Old Testament, since at that time there was no New Testament scripture.

In trying to understand what is meant by scripture being inspired, we are confronted with stories in scripture that are not at all inspiring, nor do they seem to come from God. This made me wonder whether everything in scripture is to be understood as having been dictated by God, or were just certain messages in the various books inspired by God, and thus should be taken literally? Should the rest, originating in the mind of the human author, be understood differently? In the Hebrew scriptures, it is confusing to sort out what is inspired from what is not inspired, what are the messages coming from God and what are just human recountings of a historical event or even tales passed on among the people as they sat around campfires retelling to their children stories of times past. When a story speaks of God as having slain twenty thousand people because they disobeyed Him, it makes God look like a monster. Learning how ancient Israelites interpreted natural events as expressions of God's moods helps us to realize that God was not the cause of the people dying; it was probably due to a pestilence or epidemic of some sort. Unfortunately, people who believe in the literal meaning of the scriptures accept just what is written and believe that it was God punishing the people for their sins. Interpreted literally, the scriptures portray a God who is paranoid. This does not do justice to God. Yet that is the God so many people today believe in, even though Jesus Himself portrayed an entirely different image: God as a kind, gentle, and forgiving Father. Accepting all scripture as inspired and as the sole rule of faith can leave people confused as to what to believe about God as well as about the conflicting teachings on moral issues. People who do this tend to merge Old Testament teachings with New Testament teachings, ending up with a religion that is still more confusing.

It doesn't make sense to believe that every story and event recorded in scripture should be given equal importance, as if they all contain secret messages from God. The one overpowering message of the Hebrew scriptures is that God had a special predilection for the children of Abraham, Isaac, and Jacob, and had a special purpose in calling them together as a nation. After all, what other family in the history of the human race held so tightly together for hundreds of years until the descendants bonded into a nation? The uniqueness and the rare chance of something like that happening speak volumes about God nurturing this people in spite of their many betrayals of His love and tender care. That alone is a powerful message. There are also hidden in stories and prophecies hints of future happenings and of the coming of a Savior not just for God's people but for all the nations of the world, "a light to the gentiles," as Isaiah said. God put up with all the Israelites' infidelities and betrayals because He needed them for a mission that would not be allowed to fail. God was persistent and tolerant not for them, but to assure the redemptive destiny of the human race, which was the purpose of the Messiah's coming into the world.

God prepared the people through what are called prophecies, which were interspersed throughout various books of the Hebrew Bible. Taken together, they portray a simple but graphic biographical sketch of the Messiah. They also paint a rosy picture of life when the Messiah conquers the world, a picture to capture the imagination of the people—a picture that was symbolic of supernatural victories and of life filled with spiritual delights and treasures. The people and even the religious leaders interpreted this symbolic depiction as a material paradise on earth for the Jewish people alone.

It was prophesied that this Messiah would be born of a virgin ("maiden" is the word used, but it was interpreted by the scribes as "virgin") and would come from the tribe of Judah, the tree of Jesse, and the house of David. He would be born in Bethlehem in forty week years (490 years from the ending of the Babylonian exile, which actually happened) and would be called Wonder-Counselor, Prince of Peace, Emmanu-el (God among us). It is clear that God was preparing His people for the coming of His Son, so that when He came, they would recognize Him, embrace Him, and introduce Him to the whole gentile world. Could the story of the Hebrew Bible then simply be God continually steering this people, as rebellious and difficult as they were in their relationship with Him, on a steady course until they had accomplished the task for which He had chosen them and had been preparing them for those hundreds of years? That would make sense to me. God did promise Abraham centuries before that he would be the father of many nations. If the Jewish people accepted the Messiah, their religion would have been preeminent and, like the Catholic Church, would have spread to every nation in the world. In this way God's promise to

Abraham that he would be the father of many nations would have been fulfilled.

I was having difficulty understanding how many other things in the Hebrew Bible could be inspired. Many teachings and sayings seemed ungodly. The sayings of Ecclesiastes presented a particular difficulty. I could not imagine the cynicism expressed in that book to have been inspired by God, and no matter what spin a reader might put on it, the book still expresses a cynicism about life that is unworthy of God. The final words before the epilogue are "'Sheer futility,' Qoheleth says, 'everything is futile.'"

I was beginning to understand that there were many things in the Bible that were a recounting of past events that in themselves may not have been inspired because often they were not even accurate. The evil and shameful deeds by supposedly good people seemed not things that God would have inspired. Attributing to God the orders for Joshua to destroy the people already living in the Promised Land does not seem inspired. It does not make sense that the God who forbade murder would order the destruction of a whole nation to make room for others when there was plenty of room for both to live in neighboring or divided territories, as they ultimately did. Even in my later years I still had problems accepting everything in the Bible as inspired by God. I asked myself: Why does *everything* in the Bible have to be considered inspired; why not consider as inspired just the messages that God is trying to teach us?

Another hurdle presented itself concerning the authorship of the first five books of the Bible, the Torah. For centuries Christians looked on the Torah as having been written by Moses. Even the Vatican insisted that Catholics accept that the first five books of the Old Testament were authored by Moses, and Catholic scholars were forbidden to disagree with that promulgation. But now, over a half century later, Catholics agree, as do most scripture scholars, that they were written not by Moses but by priests and scribes who wrote down stories and teachings that had originated with Moses but had been passed on from one generation to the next. Even the stories of Job and Jonah are widely accepted now not as historically true but, rather, as tales with inspired messages. For centuries they had been accepted as historical. With advances in our understanding of ancient literature and the various styles of writing at the time, they are considered allegorical. Only some fundamentalists, who insist on the literal interpretation of the Bible, believe that the stories really took place, that Jonah was swallowed by a whale or some huge seafaring animal and thrown up on a shore three days later, and that all Job's misfortunes and the theological discussions concerning those misfortunes really took place and that, in the end, all was restored to him.

I think that scripture scholars and the Church have still much to consider concerning the scriptures, including just what is inspired. In the meantime, I can feel comfortable with the realization that the Hebrew scriptures tell us much about God that we could not learn from any other source and that God does speak to us through those scriptures, even though it often may be difficult to understand precisely what it is that God is trying to tell us. The scriptures are still a precious treasure of inspired gems.

When it comes to the New Testament, there is, as in the

Hebrew scriptures, a multitude of considerations. Where did the New Testament come from? Who wrote it? Is it historically accurate? Is it inspired? Who with authority said it is inspired? The answer to *this* question is critical. The New Testament would lose much of its significance if a religious authority did not declare its contents inspired. People readily declare many literary masterpieces inspired, but no one has to believe it because there is no authority certifying that they are inspired. Saint Augustine said he accepted the Bible and the New Testament as the inspired word of God "because the Church told me so."

The New Testament is, just like the Old Testament, a collection of books, some written by apostles or by disciples close to them, others written by authors respected by the earliest Christians. The gospels' authors were not all apostles. Matthew and John were; Luke and Mark were not.

I had no problem accepting Matthew's and John's gospels. They were apostles and had Jesus' authority to teach. But Luke and Mark? Why should I accept them as inspired? They were not apostles and had no mandate from Jesus to go out and teach with Jesus' guarantee of divine guidance. The other books of the New Testament were mostly letters from the apostles to the churches they founded and were still nurturing. The Acts of the Apostles was simple enough. It is a short history written by Luke of the beginnings of the Church. The Book of Revelation was supposedly written by John or, under his guidance, by some of his learned disciples. Was it an allegory of the history of the times, or was it intended to be prophetic of events to take place in the future, even the distant future? Was it the pious dream of a saintly old man? Or was it, perhaps, an expression of the hopes and fears of a far-seeing mystic considering in his old age the future of his life's God-given mission? It was, and still is, confusing.

To know how to handle this was very difficult for me. None of the New Testament would have value if Jesus was not real and was not a divine person. Those issues had to be grappled with before anything else concerning the written word. Was Jesus a myth? The gospels tell of Mary having been visited by an angel who announced that she was to become the mother of the Son of God. Some ridicule the story as a myth, but the later unfolding of Jesus' life, manifesting so graphically the divine presence in His person and in all He did, proves the divine origin of His conception and birth. In theology courses we discussed writers who debunked the life of Jesus as myth concocted by deluded followers who had a personal stake in portraying Him as a real person. As little was mentioned about Him in secular writing of the time, most belief in Jesus had to be based on the testimony of the gospel writers. But how could they be credible if there was only scant mention of Him in secular literature?

True, testimony from secular literature was sparse, but what is mentioned did have solid value. Pliny the Elder, a Roman historian, mentions a certain Chrestus who had followers among the Jews, but was crucified. This seemed believable enough to be referring to Jesus. The Jewish historian of the time of Jesus, Josephus, speaks of Jesus at length and discusses him as a real person who had to be reckoned with by the chief priests and by the Roman governor. Although Josephus was looked on by the Jews as a turncoat because he was friendly with the Romans, and was made an official in Palestine after the fall of Jerusalem in A.D. 70, his *History of the Jews* was looked on as credible and is still used today for insights into the times. That seemed sufficient for me to accept Jesus as a real person, although I would have felt more comfortable if there were other sources as well.

My next problem was to ascertain whether the gospels were conscientiously written to portray honestly the life of Jesus, or whether they were written to win the confidence of naïve people Jesus' followers were trying to bring into their new organization so it could grow. Over this issue I struggled to determine whether the gospel writers were honest or hucksters starting a religion business. This was painful and took many years for me to be totally convinced. As I read and reread the gospels, an understanding and sense of the mentality of the gospel writers grew on me. It was not a rational conviction resulting from textual analysis or from any other intellectual exercise. It was almost like working daily with people on a job. After a while you sense whom you can trust and whom you know for a certainty to be dishonest or unworthy of your trust. I had become so familiar with the gospels, and with the thinking of the authors and the people they were writing about, it was like living with them. In this way I finally felt comfortable with the authors (or originators, if the evangelists' disciples did the actual writing) of the gospels as trustworthy. I learned to see how simple they were and how lacking they were in that certain cunning needed to spin a long, extended tale, making someone into something he was not or portraying him with an image far removed from his real life. They did not even check each other's writings to see if they were contradicting each other. Also, there were too many people who had been with Jesus and knew Him quite intimately, and had sacrificed life, friends, and possessions to follow His teachings. They would not tolerate a fraudulent portrait of someone they knew only too well. There was too much at stake for them to allow His image to be tampered with.

Most modern scripture scholars are willing to accept the gospels as essentially truthful, if not historically precise in our understanding of history. I now had enough confidence in what I was reading in the gospels to take the words and actions of Jesus at face value and use them in understanding His life and teachings and the purpose of His mission. I could accept Jesus as a well-balanced human being, highly intelligent, with a clear and penetrating vision of the purpose of human life, and I could accept that He was the fulfillment of the ancient prophecies about the Messiah. I was convinced He was not only sane but of the highest integrity and vision, with a message that was revolutionary and sublime. I was convinced He really saw happy events, and misfortune as well, not in the light of their immediate effect on a person's life here in this life but in relation to a life hereafter. This is what made Jesus' vision unique from what had been a universal philosophy embracing only this life and our quality of life here. Jesus viewed this life as momentary and transitory and weighed everything in its relationship to life to come when this life is finished. So He could say, with utter sincerity, to desperately poor people, "Blessed are you poor in spirit; you will one day possess the kingdom of heaven." The fact that He could say with such conviction that the poor need not be overly concerned about their life of want here on earth, for one day they will be richly rewarded in heaven for what they have endured in this life, made Him believable even to the poor and the destitute. When He talked about the other world, His Father's home, He spoke of it as if He had lived there. No one ever talked like that before. No one ever talked about heaven before. It was never discussed, because no one knew anything about the place. Jesus talked about it in a casual manner as a familiar reality. He was not offering proofs of heaven's existence, but talked about it as if it were an address just around the corner and He knew the way there. I was now ready to accept Jesus for who He said He was, the Son of God, one with the Father, and equal to the Father, and with whom the Father shares all things.

I finally reached the starting line, the beginning of what my religion was supposed to be all about. I was on the threshold of understanding the reality of Jesus and who He was and what He meant to humanity. He was, by His Father's decree, the center of human existence, the beginning and end of all creation, the Alpha and the Omega. If Isaiah was right, Jesus was, as the prophet said, "Emmanu-el," "God living among us." Jesus was, then, central to the destiny of the human race. He could never be considered just one of many options. He was, by the will of the Creator, the whole reason for human existence, the only one who could give meaning and direction to human life on earth; the only one who could promise heaven to those who were willing to follow Him, because it was His home, and only He could invite creatures to His eternal home.

Now that the Son of God had come down to earth, what

was the purpose of His coming? What was His life all about? Why was He sharing His life with His creatures? What a comedown! What humility! What was it He intended to share? That led me to the study of Jesus Himself and what His purpose was in coming to earth.

6

JESUS, EMMANU-EL

*t*HE FIRST THIRTY YEARS of Jesus' life on earth seemed not to have been spectacular, considering who He was and what His life could have been. He was born of parents who were descendants of highly respected but impoverished royal and priestly families. Shortly after His birth, a crazed king, jealous of his throne, tried to assassinate the child, so the family fled as refugees to Egypt. On their return, years later, they settled in an inconspicuous village in Galilee, named Nazareth, where they spent the next twenty to twenty-five years as simple folk who made little impression on the other villagers, other than for their goodness and simplicity of life.

It was not until Jesus was thirty years old that people began to understand that there was something extraordinary about Him. He had just returned from a journey to Jerusalem, where He met His cousin, John, the son of a priest named Zechariah and his wife, Elizabeth. John had been preaching the impending coming of the long-awaited Savior and had been calling the people to repentance by submitting to his baptism. Jesus asked John to baptize Him. After protesting that Jesus should be baptizing him, John finally relented and performed the baptism. The people nearby sensed that something extraordinary was happening but did not understand its significance.

After emerging from the baptism, Jesus left the scene and was followed by two men who happened to be from Galilee. One was named Andrew, the brother of a fisherman named Simon. Jesus turned to see who was following Him and said, "What do you want?"

"Where do you live?" was their response.

Jesus told them, "Come and see."

That was an interesting response because Jesus did not live in Judea, where they were at the time, so he could not have brought them to His home. He may have had friends or relatives who lived locally. If the men stayed with Jesus, they probably ended up sleeping in a grove of trees on the bank of the Jordan River, or they could have gone down farther south and ended up at Qumran, with the Jewish reformers there who were anxiously awaiting the coming of the Messiah.

The gospel continues with Jesus being driven by the Spirit to retreat into the desert in an area between Jericho and Qumran. He spent the next forty days in caves on the cliff overlooking Jericho.

After that retreat He emerged fortified and inspired by the Spirit to begin His ministry. Jesus began by preaching and talking about the kingdom of heaven, whose coming

John preached. Apparently He performed some deeds that impressed the bystanders, because word quickly reached Nazareth, and the townsfolk were ready for him on His return there a few days later.

That return to Nazareth was devastating. The townsfolk were offended to learn that Jesus was preaching and blessing people with His healing power. After all, He had never done anything like that in His hometown. Their reaction was expressed in their comments to one another: "Where did he get all this from? Isn't this the carpenter's son, whom we grew up with, and whose family we all know?"

Jesus had been with them for all those years, and they never saw anything unusual about Him. Now they were jealous that he should work wonders elsewhere. So, when Jesus spoke in their synagogue, He brought up the issue. He was presented with the scroll and, after reading from the prophet Isaiah, He declared that Isaiah's prophecy about the Messiah was being fulfilled in their very sight. He ended by saying, "No doubt you will say to me, 'Physician, heal yourself! Do here the things we have heard you have done in other places! But, I tell you, I cannot do those things here, because you do not believe in me.'"

Insulted, they dragged Him out of the synagogue and drove Him from town. From that day on, He never returned. The congregation had totally missed the unique honor Jesus showed them by announcing to them first that He was their long-awaited Messiah.

Jesus then began preaching in Capernaum. Shortly afterward, He and his new disciples were invited to a wedding party at the little village of Cana. From close reading of the gospel account, it seems that the family may have been relatives or at least very close friends of Jesus and His mother, because we find Mary working behind the scenes, and she is the one who noticed that the wine had run out. Apparently Joseph was dead by that time; there is no mention of him.

As soon as Jesus arrives, three days late, with His newfound disciples, His mother tells Him that the wine has run out. Obviously she is hinting that He do something about it, because Jesus complains that the time appointed by His Father to work miracles has not yet come.

However, because His mother asked Him, Jesus worked His first miracle by changing close to 180 gallons of water into the choicest wine. That was Jesus' official inauguration of His mission. The gospel writer expressed it very succinctly: "This was the first of Jesus' miracles." It is interesting that it was at a wedding party, and Jesus' first official act was to miraculously provide barrels of wine to a couple whose wedding party was about to be cut short by a shortage of wine. How earthy, and yet how beautiful, for Jesus to start His ministry in such a compassionate manner, immediately defining the simple, tender way the Father views His human children.

It was important for me to concentrate on Jesus' messages and how He intended to execute His role as Messiah. The Jewish people expected a military leader who would come and defeat all Israel's enemies and begin a thousand years of prosperity and power for Israel. From the start of Jesus' ministry it was clear from His awesome powers—His healing powers and His ability to even raise the dead back to life—that He would be an ideal messianic leader. His army would be invincible. Who would be foolish enough to even think of opposing it?

The interesting thing is, even though Jesus would not be a worldly messiah, the promises to Israel would still be true. If the Jewish leaders accepted Jesus, the Christian community would not have had to split from Judaism. The Jews would not have revolted against Rome. Jerusalem would have been the head of the newly transformed religion that had accepted its messiah, and as the Jewish apostles brought the message of Jesus to the whole world, Jerusalem would have become the center of a religion that had conquered the world. The promise that God made to Abraham long ago would have been fulfilled; he would indeed be the father of many nations.

Did Jesus have all the powers that are attributed to Him in the gospels? Just because the gospels say so was not convincing enough for me, though they do show the Pharisees themselves not denying Jesus' miraculous powers but instead attributing them to the power of the devil. Even so, I would have felt more comfortable if there was evidence from sources outside the gospels. I needed a more objective testimony. There was nothing in Roman history or literature of the time. But, surprisingly, Jewish literature reluctantly records and discusses the issue. The miracles of Jesus were a phenomenon the Jewish writers would have liked to just dismiss as rumor, but so many Jewish people witnessed His miracles that the writers of the Talmud later on could not deny them, but attributed them to sorcery Jesus brought with him from Egypt—whenever he was supposed to have been in Egypt.

Realizing that even Jesus' enemies could not deny the fact of His miracles, I was now willing to read the story of the cures and healings and accept them. However, the cases of demonic possession seemed to be a different issue. I could accept demonic possession, and Jesus' healing of those genuinely possessed, but I also felt that some of the incidents involved psychological or emotional abnormalities, or epilepsy. I could identify with the case of the man possessed, whose evil spirit said his name was Legion because they were many, because I had run into a similar case of a person with a multiple personality problem where the voice said the same thing with a variation: "You think there are three of us, don't you? There are not three of us. There are five of us." The person from whom this voice came was sound asleep, and the voice was nothing like the person's true voice.

Since the miracles no longer presented a problem for me, I felt I could move on to analyzing the teachings of Jesus. This was to turn out to be a difficult task, as Jesus did not spell out in orderly fashion the purpose of His life and teachings, the way a philosopher or theologian would present ideas. The reader has to pick out of Jesus' many talks, which were only briefly and sketchily recorded, individual ideas and try to put them together like pieces of a puzzle in a way that makes sense. Maybe that was the way Jesus spoke. Maybe He did not speak in long, logical discourses, explaining the rationale behind His mission. Perhaps He did, but the gospel writers either did not remember it all or did not at the time understand what He was talking about. They do not appear to have been intellectually inclined or even deep thinkers. At any rate, the fact that they did not record Jesus' talks as logical, systematic discourses was one of the reasons that convinced me that the evangelists were not trying to convince their readers of anything, just recording sketchy memories for those who already loved Jesus. For a person who was trying to understand and make sense of Him, this was exasperating.

I had to go through the gospels and try to determine which ideas would seem to be the starting point of what Jesus saw as His mission and what He was expecting of the people. Did He look on Himself as the Messiah everyone expected, or did He have His own understanding of the Messiah's mission? He kept saying, "I have come to do the will of my Father." What *was* the Father's will? Was it the Father's dream that His Son be a military genius to lead one human family to conquer and subdue all others? Or was God concerned about the human family's relationship with Himself, which had been ruptured and shattered in times long past? What was this will of His Father to which Jesus was so devoted?

He made a remark one day, "I have come to set fire on the earth, and what would I but that it be enkindled?" A fire! For what purpose? An overpowering passion for some goal perhaps, but the gospel writer never finished the thought, so the reader is left dangling as to what that goal was. "Come to me," He once said, "all you who are weary and heavily burdened and I will refresh you, for my yoke is easy and my burden light," and "Learn from me, for I am meek and humble of heart," but neither statement seems to fully answer the question.

Why were these trains of thought never completed? To what purpose was this strange Messiah continually calling these people? Did He ever lay down in precise and clear terms the purpose of His mission? The answer is no. At the very beginning of His ministry, Jesus called men to follow him. "Come, follow me, and I will make you fishers of human beings," he said to Simon, Andrew, James, and John as they were working on the nets in their fishing boats. They left all and followed Him for the rest of their lives. They followed Him to fish for human beings. What were they to do with these human beings when they caught them?

As time passed, it became clear that Jesus was not in the slightest bit interested in a worldly kingdom. He kept talking about a kingdom of heaven, which confused the people. What kind of a messiah is this? What's this kingdom He is talking about? A kingdom of heaven! What's a kingdom of heaven? No one has ever heard of such a place called heaven. What's this heaven all about?

Jesus never was specific. When people asked Him to explain further, He told them parables. "The kingdom of heaven is like a man in search of fine pearls. One day he found a really valuable pearl, and sold everything he had to possess it. Or again, the kingdom of heaven is like a man who found a treasure hidden in a field. He sold everything he had to buy that field." His answer seems vague. Maybe it was intentionally vague, or maybe the gospel writer never properly transcribed the whole of Jesus' conversation. But when Jesus spoke about this kingdom of heaven, He did have a brutally realistic understanding of what it would be like. Even though in one sentence He calls it the pearl of great price, in the next sentence he compares it to a catch of fish. "The kingdom of heaven is like a fisherman who went out and caught a huge draught of fish. Sitting on the shore he separated the good from the bad. The good ones he put into pails. The rotten fish he disposed of."

It is becoming clear that this kingdom of heaven is people, the people who commit themselves to follow Jesus. Now, what is this kingdom like? What is its purpose, and where is this kingdom? "The kingdom of heaven is within you," Jesus told them. He did not tell them what this kingdom is all about. He did not tell them He was not the kind of messiah they were expecting. That would have been a fatal mistake. Since the people had been misled by their religious leaders, who themselves had misunderstood the prophets' teaching about the messianic kingdom, Jesus could not have come out and denied it. He had to painstakingly try to interest the people into thinking of the possibility of another and more wonderful kingdom. It was a risky strategy, but one He had to resort to since the religious leaders failed in their own mission to prepare the people properly.

Some of the more spiritually minded who were deeply affected by Jesus' idea of a heavenly kingdom embraced His message. For example, Mary and Martha were taken up with His idea of resurrection to a new life after death. Many, however, just walked away—until they wanted something, such as a healing for a friend or family member. Then they might come back temporarily for a healing, for which Jesus apparently never said no.

Even intelligent and spiritual persons had problems with Jesus' talk about being saved. Nicodemus, a member of the seventy-two-man Sanhedrin that ruled Jerusalem, came to Jesus late at night and asked what he must do to be saved. Jesus told him that he must be born again.

"Born again? I am an old man. How can I be born again?"

Jesus told him he must be born again spiritually. "Be baptized and receive the Holy Spirit and you will be born to new life, and when you die you will enter the kingdom of heaven."

Now Jesus is introducing another facet of God, a Holy Spirit. "Unless you are born of water and the Holy Spirit you cannot have life in you."

Baptism, then, is initiation into this kingdom that the

Messiah is setting up. So, that is the kingdom. Not a kingdom of this world but a kingdom that belongs to another world, a world in another dimension of reality, the world where God lives. Now, if that was real, that could be exciting. But that idea was far removed from the dream of the Jewish people. They knew of no other world. How could Jesus make that world real to them? He kept trying slowly and patiently. Gradually more and more people, convinced of His sincerity, were willing to commit themselves to Him. Paradoxically, once John the Baptizer was executed by Herod, Jesus' family began to grow in large numbers.

7

ORGANIZING THE NEW KINGDOM

As JOHN'S FOLLOWERS WENT OVER to Jesus and others began to believe in Him, Jesus' ministry went into high gear. He and His disciples were now baptizing greater numbers and gathering people together as a community, teaching them that they now shared one life and were bonded to each other as a family. No longer was the Jewish law, with its 613 commandments, the guiding principle of people's relationship with God; now their caring for one another was evidence of the sincerity of their love for God. "A new commandment I give you, that you love one another as I have loved you." And as the ultimate expression of that love, "Greater love than this no one has than that he or she is willing to lay down their life for a friend," which was also a reference to His laying down His life for the human race. And as the only hint as to how our eternal fate will be decided at the Last Judgment, Jesus tells His followers:

When the Son of Man comes to judge, he will separate the sheep from the goats. He will place the sheep on his right hand and say to them, "Come, blessed of my Father, into the Kingdom prepared for you from the beginning of time. When I was hungry, you gave me food. When I was thirsty, you gave me drink. When I was naked, you clothed me. When I was ill, you cared for me. When I was in prison, you came to visit me."

" 'When, Lord, did we ever see you in these straits?'

" 'As long as you did it for the least of my brothers and sisters, you did it for me.' "

Interesting. No longer was an Israelite automatically a member of this new kingdom, the kingdom of heaven, just because he was a circumcised Jew. People had to accept the kingdom. They had to commit themselves to it, by making a commitment of their lives to the King who would one day be their Judge deciding their eternal fate, eternal happiness with God in the heavenly kingdom or eternal exile from Yahweh for those who refuse to love not just God but, more particularly, human beings who desperately need love and care on this earth.

Surprisingly, this was not new. It was what Yahweh had been promising for ages through the prophets. The religious leaders, in their spiritual bankruptcy, had failed to understand this and, even more disastrously, had failed to teach their people, so no one could understand the kind of kingdom that Jesus preached about. Strangely enough, I thought, we run the same risk today as Christians. As the Jewish religious leaders of times past centered their lives on the institution and its ancient customs, which took on the aura of the sacred, so religious life of Christians is centered on the institution, as Jesus is all but forgotten. There is hardly a seminary, Catholic or Protestant, that teaches candidates for ministry about Jesus, other than a sketchy course in Christology, which is little more than a short history of the development of doctrine concerning Jesus, the God-Man. As far as teaching in depth about Jesus—what He was like as a person, how He treated all kinds of people, sinners as well as righteous people, and how His acceptance of sinners was so radically different from the way the scribes and Pharisees and priests treated sinners—that kind of teaching is sadly lacking. As a result, clergy go out into their ministries with only a shallow idea of Jesus and little awareness of how He, the Good Shepherd, would treat people who have serious problems. They often treat troubled and hurting people and people emotionally and psychologically damaged from childhood with a rudeness and lack of compassion that is shocking. It seems they have never met the Jesus who could preach the highest of ideals, but show exquisite compassion when He met a sinner who fell far short of those ideals. This kind of treatment by so many clergy pained me deeply, especially when I came across so much human anguish left in the wake of these insensitive shepherds. I knew something had to be seriously lacking either in the clergy or in their training for the problem to be so widespread.

Caring for others was central to Jesus' message. For that reason, many people accepted His teaching and followed Him, often at great cost to themselves, as many lost family and loved ones. In time this group that gathered around Him became a family of people who cared. This was revolutionary, because it was intimate. For Jesus no one was a stranger, and when He accepted them into His family, from then on none of them was a stranger to the others. This was real family, not just make-believe. They were expected to treat each other like family members, sharing what they had with each other and being there for each other when they were needed.

This was a radical departure from the religion they were familiar with. Hospitality was important to the Jewish people, but this was true intimacy. It involved the establishment of relationships and responsibility for one another. As the family grew, Jesus then began to organize. He needed people, special people He would train to carry on His work when He should die. For this work He chose twelve, whom he called apostles. They became His closest confidants with whom He shared everything. As time passed and He knew the end of His life on earth was approaching, He called them aside and gave them their mission: "Go out and teach the whole world. Teach them all that I have taught you. Those who accept you accept me. Those who refuse to accept you refuse to accept me." And also He promised the unerring guidance of the Holy Spirit: "I will send the Holy Spirit to be with you always, to bring back to your minds all that I have taught you. And I will be with you until the end of time." To one of those apostles, Simon, He said, after his God had given Simon a special revelation as to Jesus' identity as the Son of God: "Blessed are you, Simon, son of John, because flesh and blood has not revealed this to you, but my Father in heaven. And I say to you, 'You are Rock, and on this Rock I will build my Church, and the gates of hell [error and falsehood] shall not prevail against it.' And I give to you the keys of the kingdom of heaven.

Whatsoever you will bind on earth, I will bind in heaven, and whatsoever you will loose on earth, I will loose in heaven."

That was at last something definite, something I could hang on to. Jesus was laying the foundation for the kingdom of heaven on earth. Simon was the rock foundation and head of the band of specially chosen apostles. This was the beginning of the establishment of the new kingdom. These men whom He picked to carry on His work would continue their mission until the end of time. It was not that they would live forever, but they would live on through those they would choose specially to pass on the power Jesus gave them, as the power of Moses was passed on to each succeeding generation of Jewish religious leaders, to teach and feed the flock after them. In this way Jesus assured the continuation of His mission to all generations until the end of the world. It was simple but effective. This orderly passing on of apostleship with the authority to teach and the power to perform Baptism, the Eucharist, and confer the Holy Spirit, as well as ordaining successors in their ministry, was essential for the continuation of Jesus' ministry. There was no provision for individuals to go off on their own and pass themselves off as divinely appointed apostles. The guarantee of the integrity of His message as it was transmitted from one generation to the next was assured as Jesus promised to send the Holy Spirit to be with the apostles, not just anyone who wanted to preach, until the end of time. The Holy Spirit would be with the apostles and their successors to bring back to their minds all the things that Jesus taught them. If people were required to accept Jesus and His teachings, Jesus had the obligation to guarantee the faithful transmission of those teachings forever. His establishing

Simon as the Rock on which He would build His church added to that guarantee, especially as He promised that hell itself would never succeed in destroying or distorting His message when taught by the apostles and their successors.

Later on, before moving on to other cities, Paul chose Timothy to succeed him in Ephesus. Paul laid his hands on Timothy and called down upon him the Holy Spirit, the ritual by which the apostles passed on to those succeeding them the authority and power Jesus had given to them. In this way the directive of Jesus was fulfilled to go and teach all nations until the end of time.

All these things I could understand. They made sense. If Jesus wanted His message to be taught in its integrity to all generations, He had to guarantee its faithful transmission so the same message would be available to all people forever, a seeming impossibility, but possible only if God guaranteed it.

Besides the twelve apostles, Jesus chose another seventy-two as assistants to send ahead to other villages and towns and prepare the way for His coming to preach His message. There may not have been a complex organization at that point. It was not yet needed. Considering the small size of the community, however, it was a well-organized system, sufficient for its needs at that time. Built into that simple structure was its dynamic for continuity and further development.

The concept of family, which was so important to Jesus, was further developed on the occasion of His speaking to the large crowd that followed Him across the lake one day. He had tried to escape so the apostles could have some quality time alone with Him. When they arrived at the opposite shore, they found that the crowd had run around the lake and was waiting for Him. Jesus' only comment was "I feel sorry for the people. They are like sheep without a shepherd."

Jesus spoke to them again for a long time, and then, concerned that it was getting late and they had not eaten, he told the apostles to break them into groups of fifty and a hundred and seat them along the hillside. Then, finding a boy with a few loaves and fishes, Jesus multiplied them and, like a family on picnic, fed the whole crowd. His actions, however, seemed to have another lesson and another kind of food in mind, which He intended to share with them the next day.

Arriving at the opposite shore the next morning, and seeing the same people gathering, Jesus promised them a food that would prepare them for eternal life. This food was His own flesh and blood, which He would give them in a way that demanded great faith in Him. Not able to understand what He was promising, they walked away in disbelief. Surely He would not give them His own flesh and blood as the food for their souls. Even Moses could not give their ancestors food to guarantee eternal life. What Jesus was promising was ridiculous. He had gone too far, and they left in disgust.

What Jesus did not tell them was something that would have made sense for them. He demanded *faith* from them, and He had given them plenty of reasons to believe Him. It was not until the night of the Passover, when He was celebrating the official sacrificial meal of the Old Testament, that Jesus instituted the official sacrificial meal of the New Testament in His flesh and blood, when He took the bread and wine and gave it to His disciples with the words "Take and eat. This is my body which will be given up for you." Then with the cup, He said, "Take and drink. This is the cup of my blood, the blood of the new and eternal covenant, which will be shed for you and for all for the forgiveness of sins."

Another intimate family meal. In this mystical meal Jesus created a new type of presence, a presence more intimate than His presence throughout the universe, a presence that brings to those who open their hearts to receive Him comfort and strength, and Jesus' pledge of eternal life. After sharing this gift of life with the apostles, Jesus told them to continue renewing this gift after His departure from them, which they did faithfully every Sunday evening after His Ascension.

As dark as was the depression that veiled my faith, I never had a difficulty embracing this gift of Jesus in the Eucharist. I looked forward to my daily Communion. I knew that some Christians of other denominations considered Communion merely a symbol of Jesus' presence. This I could not understand. For me what Jesus said seemed clear: "Unless you eat my flesh and drink my blood you cannot have eternal life." The earliest Christians taught by the apostles accepted that literal meaning of Jesus' words. They treasured the real presence of Jesus in their "breaking of bread." Saint Ignatius, the successor of Peter as bishop of Antioch, who was revered by the earliest Christians as having been with Jesus as a youth (he was probably in his teens when he met Jesus), made it clear that the Eucharist embodied the real presence of Jesus. In writing to one of the Christian communities after celebrating the Eucharist with them on his way to Rome for his martyrdom, he complains how sad it was that some Christians no longer believed that Jesus was present in the Eucharist. That was as early as the year A.D. 105. Ignatius also criticized the Gnostics for not believing the Eucharist to be the flesh and blood of Jesus Christ. Other early Church fathers believed as Ignatius did. Saint Justin, for example, wrote that "the food we receive that is blessed by the prayer of His word is the flesh and blood of Jesus."

The Eucharist was my one powerful support during the frightening years of my depression. And though I did not have the emotional consolations I had always experienced as a young boy, I drew strength from my daily contact with Jesus in Communion. Reading the Fathers of the Church reinforced my attachment, knowing that their faith came from the apostles themselves, who knew the mind of Jesus. This is why I had such a hard time understanding how some Protestant groups could so easily reject such a beautiful gift of Jesus, especially since that belief was so strongly held by Christians taught by the apostles.

This eternal life that Jesus promised to those who would take up their cross and follow Him—that fascinated me. This eternal life. What did Jesus mean by it? Would it be life on earth forever? He said on one occasion, "In my Father's house there are many places to live. I go to prepare a place for you, so that where I am there you also may be."

So, this eternal life was someplace else. It was not here. Where was it? What is this life, this eternal life, the kingdom of heaven that is not on earth? Paradise, Jesus called it when He promised the repentant thief on the cross that he would be there with Him that very day.

About this paradise He said, "The eye has not seen, nor has the ear ever heard, nor has it ever entered the human imagination the wonderful things my Father has prepared for those who love him." Everything is still mysterious. Is there another world beyond this one? People always talked about heaven being up and hell being down. Down is in the center of the earth. Heaven—does that mean up in the air?

I now knew that Jesus promised heaven to those who would follow Him. But I could not pin down in my mind what or where this place was, if indeed it was a place and not just a psychological state of some kind. At least Jesus taught about heaven. To understand this more fully meant further struggling later on for its meaning and how it could make sense to me. All anyone seemed to know about heaven was that people there played musical instruments, harps and trumpets and violins, and sang hymns. All of this really left me cold, and rather frightened; is that all there is to do for all eternity? That subject needed a lot more thought if it was to make sense to me or even be appealing. I certainly did not want to spend my eternity singing hymns and playing harps. From what little I already had learned about Jesus, He did not strike me as the kind of person who would enjoy spending his time doing that either. I was beginning to see Jesus as a humble person who enjoyed companionship and doing good things for others; he did not look for praise and personal glory. But that was for later study. There were too many other things that needed more immediate attention before I could become obsessed with the details of life in heaven. And later on it became an obsession. I eventually had to know as much as I could about life in heaven and what life there was all about, and whether it could really be enjoyable and appealing, or endlessly boring. Suffice it to say that, at this point, God did not impress me as the kind of person who would enjoy people just standing around singing and saying nice things about Him, like some Roman emperor or Oriental potentate. If He's God, He doesn't need or even desire that stuff.

It finally struck me that in telling His disciples about the kingdom of heaven on earth and the kingdom of heaven where His Father dwelt, Jesus summed up the purpose of all His teachings. It was a package He was offering, a well-constructed way of life with a long-term purpose and goal. It was now up to the people to decide whether this was appealing to them and something they were willing to give all they had in order to accept. Jesus promised a life after death where there would be no more tears, no more sadness, but peace and happiness for all eternity. No one had ever spelled it out like that before. Could this very saintly prophet deliver on what He was promising? Was He believable? How could He guarantee what He was promising? It seems not too many people were willing to make that commitment. Those who still had strong doubts would wait until other events took place in Jesus' life that impressed them.

8

THE RAISING OF LAZARUS

As I BECAME MORE FAMILIAR with the gospel events—not just from one gospel but from gathering together events recorded in all the gospels—it struck me that there is a logical progression embedded in the story of Jesus' life. This progression made me realize how much Jesus was in control of His own destiny. The gospel episodes may appear disjointed and disconnected, but there is an inner logic to what is happening as Jesus' life unfolds. The gospel writers themselves may not have even been aware of it, but the events are not haphazard, nor are they really disjointed. Reading carefully, we can see that Jesus is moving steadily and inevitably in the direction He chooses toward the goal decided by Him and His Father long ago. This is very evident in the drama over Lazarus' mortal illness and Jesus' awareness of it, and the perfect timing of His arrival at Mary and Martha's house for the mourning ceremony. It is also significant that Jesus is keenly aware that His own life is coming to a close, as He carefully orchestrates each of the daily events leading up to that final drama. He is also aware that the apostles needed a deeper reason to have faith in His promises, a faith that would be strong enough to inspire them to make the sacrifices necessary to embrace that difficult cross entailed in following Him. The next episode unfolded for their benefit.

Before leaving to visit Martha and Mary in Bethany, Jesus was spending time with the apostles, in no apparent hurry to leave. He mentioned to them that Lazarus was very sick. The apostles were naturally concerned and wondered why Jesus was so casual about it, making no attempt to visit their sick friend. After all, the apostles were also Lazarus's friends. Then Jesus said, "Lazarus is asleep. Let us go wake him." "Lord, if he is asleep, he must be getting better. Why wake him?" one apostle asked.

Then Jesus told them, "Lazarus is dead."

The apostles were even more shocked at Jesus' apparent lack of concern. Then Jesus told them that Lazarus has died for their edification, so they may better understand Jesus' power from the Father. After picking up their meager belongings, the group took off for Bethany.

I was impressed with what followed: that Jesus knew He was going to be able to raise Lazarus from the dead, and also that Mary and Martha knew that those who followed Jesus would rise to new life on the last day. That was a teaching that had not been mentioned previously in the gospels, although Jesus obviously had talked about it, at least to Mary and Martha.

The raising of Lazarus was particularly significant because of the long period of time he had been dead, four days. Jesus had previously raised from the dead people who had just died, but this was different. By this time, presumably Lazarus' body was in a state of advanced decay. This particular miracle manifests another of Jesus' powers: His power over the chemical and biological changes involved in raising a person so long dead. Either He had miraculously prevented the body from decaying, or He had the power to restore the disintegrating molecular structure of a decaying corpse.

My ability to accept the reality of Jesus' life and the authenticity of His message was not as important to me as the realization that His miracles were an authentic part of the fabric of His life, a part that even the Jewish religious leaders at the time could not deny, nor did they attempt to deny. I was reminded of the artist John Trost's approach to Jesus. What impressed John and led to his conversion was not so much the miracles, though they certainly were a powerful supporting influence, but Jesus' teachings. John told me that Jesus' teachings were so sublime, a mere human could not have invented them. Only God could teach the things that Jesus taught. How could a human promise heaven? No one even knew about the place. How could a mere human talk about the nature of God with such intimacy and reveal that the unity of God is shared by a trinity of persons? Once John realized the power and implications of Jesus' teachings, from then on he no longer had an option to accept or discard Jesus. It was a matter of conscience to accept and obey what the Creator requires of His creatures.

I was surprised that John did not seem to make as much of

the miracles as he did of Jesus' teachings. John had never had any contact with Christianity or Catholicism while a Communist in France. If he did, it was only by hearsay, and obliquely, since the God reflected in the lives of Christians he knew did not particularly impress him.

When he read the Bible and, especially, the gospels later in life, it was a fresh and uncontaminated experience. It was all totally new. We who have been Christians all our lives could never have that unadulterated understanding of scripture. When we pick up the gospels, especially for the first time, we are already programmed as to what they should mean to us or how we should view what we read. John found in the gospels a wholly new and beautiful world, so different from the life he had known and the world that Christians supposedly believed in. John's experience reinforced conclusions I had been drawing from my own search to understand the basis for belief.

What else was fascinating about Lazarus' coming back to life was a comment made in John's gospel about the religious leaders who were apparently "friends" of Lazarus' family. They had heard about the miracle and were considering killing Lazarus to destroy the evidence of Jesus' power to raise the dead. John had valuable inside information concerning this because he was on friendly terms with members of the high priest's family. He shared information from this source only rarely and discreetly.

The raising of Lazarus was a powerful experience for the apostles, crowning evidence of God's approval of Jesus' life and work.

9

THE RESURRECTION OF JESUS

*H*AVING THE POWER to raise others to life is one thing. Having the power to bring oneself back to life is something quite different. Jesus once made the remark "I have the power to lay down my life and to take it up again." He also said, "No one takes my life from me."

Interesting! Jesus is declaring that He is in total control of His own destiny. I will never forget a statement one of my theology professors made when commenting on the crucifixion and words of Jesus, "Father, into your hands I commend my spirit," and "It is finished." Then Jesus breathed forth His spirit.

"There is an important issue here," the professor told us. "This is the issue. Jesus was not killed. Jesus chose to die, and He died at the exact moment of His choosing. He offered Himself on the cross for us. He is the priest and also the victim, offering Himself to His heavenly Father to atone for our sins. When His work was finished, He spoke those words, breathed forth His spirit, and died, at the exact time He chose."

Jesus also said on a number of occasions that He would rise again. This would be the test as to whether He was in control of His life and His destiny. Apparently no one believed Him, except perhaps Caiaphas, the high priest who had remembered Jesus' threat: "Destroy this temple and in three days I will rebuild it." Caiaphas was shrewd. He took Jesus very seriously. Others may have listened to what Jesus had to say, but often they did not take Him seriously. Caiaphas took seriously everything Jesus said. If He promised to rise again, Caiaphas would take no chances. He used Jesus' promise to rise again to convince Pontius Pilate that a guard should be placed around the tomb to make sure nothing out of the ordinary happened after His burial.

The critical three days were about to begin. Jesus was buried. If He had the power to take up His life, what would He be doing during those three days before He was to rise? I was more curious than concerned for reasons of faith, but it was a question that I would have liked answered. It took a long time before I found evidence that made sense to me. First of all, part of the question was answered by Saint Peter in his first letter. He said Jesus went down to the regions below, meaning the place where the good people of the past were waiting for the good news to be announced. All the holy people of the Old Testament, as well as good people in the pagan world, whose goodness is credited to them as commitment to God, were waiting for salvation. They had waited a long time for this day. Heaven was not opened prior to Jesus' Resurrection. Jesus came to earth to win that reward for them and for us. It was the prize awaiting us as the essence of our salvation. As soon as Jesus died, he descended to the nether-world, or Hades, or limbo, or whatever name God gave it, and announced that those waiting there could now enter heaven. The good thief on the cross was also told that he would be with Jesus in paradise that very day. It was almost as if Jesus were so excited about His victory over evil that He could not wait to announce the good news to someone who was not even dead, even before He made the announcement to all those good departed souls who had been waiting for so long.

To my surprise, I did not have a difficulty approaching the resurrection of Jesus. From events in His life and His humble simplicity as He went about healing and teaching, graciously bearing rude treatment from people, I was deeply moved. This, together with the total control He had over His own destiny, which no mere human ever possessed, convinced me that if He said He had the power to take up His life after death, that was entirely believable. Jesus had foretold it, and although it was obvious that the apostles did not believe Him in the beginning, He did accomplish what He had promised, as attested by Mary and Martha, later by the two disciples on the road to Emmaus, and eventually by the apostles.

It was due principally to the stunning evidence and fact of the Resurrection that so many Pharisees and priests joined the community of believers shortly afterward. They had inside knowledge from friends within the Sanhedrin as to what actually took place on the first Easter morning. How could the sincere among them not open their hearts to Yahweh in the face of such overwhelming evidence of His endorsement of Jesus' life and message?

The next question that crossed my mind was *when* did

Jesus come back to life and rise from the dead? Was it really Easter Sunday morning? It did not make sense to me that He would hang around in a dark, empty tomb if He did not have to.

The Shroud of Turin brings to light some fascinating insights into that question. While there are some issues concerning the shroud that still must be resolved, latest evidence is very strong that it was in fact the shroud in which Jesus was buried. According to evidence from the shroud, the body was still in the state of rigor mortis or rigid state or that rigor mortis had just left the body before it left the shroud. Rigor mortis usually ceases after at most a few hours. There is no evidence on the cloth that the body had relaxed. It was still in a taut position when the body left, and there was no sign that the shroud was torn from the body. It was as if the body just passed through the shroud without altering it in the slightest way. Even the blood stains were left intact with no sign of tearing. The only phenomenon that seemed strange was the radiation burns surrounding the image of the body. What caused them? Is radiation an accidental quality of a glorified body?

While all this was not scientific evidence for me, the many details revealed in the shroud matched details in the gospel record, which was an added support.

At this point I felt secure in my acceptance that Jesus was the Messiah, the Son of God, and that He was not the type of messiah the Jewish people wanted or were even expecting. His life and teachings convinced me that He truly was a divine person and that the kingdom He came to found was an eternal kingdom open to all who were willing to accept Him, His teachings, and His way of life, and that they would one day be with Him in paradise. I could accept that He raised Lazarus from the dead and also kept His promise to rise from His own death at that first Easter. He had forever changed the destiny of the human race by making it possible for us to be no longer just God's creatures but children in God's family and heirs to His eternal kingdom of heaven. What He had accomplished as Messiah was much more than even the most fervent of Jewish dreamers expected of a messiah. Perhaps His life should be reevaluated and His case retried.

Although Saint Peter mentioned that Jesus descended into the netherworld, that event may have been before the actual Resurrection, which still may have occurred on Sunday. Jesus said He would rise after three days. No matter when it happened, it must have been a cataclysmic event. Imagine the shock of the guards! Jesus no doubt must have just passed through the tomb like a ray of light passing through a window. His glorified body could penetrate matter. Did the guards see this happening, as the apostles saw Jesus passing through the wall of their upper room? Or did they find out that Jesus rose only after the tremor or whatever it was that shook the stone away from the entrance and they could see the tomb was empty? Perhaps both events happened simultaneously. Whatever happened, the guards knew that Jesus rose from the dead, and this is what they relayed to the high priest. Scripture says that the high priest bribed the soldiers to spread the tale that they had been overcome and that the body was stolen. The truth of what happened had to have leaked out, however; that would explain why so many priests and Pharisees became disciples shortly afterward.

10

THE FIFTY DAYS
THAT FOLLOWED

SOME SIGNIFICANT THINGS HAPPENED after Jesus' Resurrection that tied together other pieces of the puzzle for me. The story about Jesus meeting the two disciples on the way to Emmaus intrigued me, especially since historians at one time ridiculed the story as fictitious, saying there was no such highway there in Jesus' day.

A number of years ago, I took my mother and father to the Holy Land. For me it was a journey of research. For my parents it was a pilgrimage of faith, a journey filled with pious expectations.

I had read for many years about the research being done in the Holy Land, especially by the Franciscans, who had been working there for centuries. One place I was particularly interested in was Emmaus. I felt Emmaus could tell a powerful story if it could be shown as historically true.

While my mother and father rested, I read a book written by a Franciscan archeologist by the name of Father Eugene Hoade, who had been working in the Holy Land all his life. I decided to follow the results of his research on the story about Emmaus and on other sites. Finding that place would have meant a lot to me. I was determined to find it even if most people were not even aware of where it was and few tours even visited the site. The first thing I learned as we drove along the back roads is that Arab villagers knew nothing about a place called Emmaus. Eventually one old man, who had lived there since childhood, told me that the place is no longer called Emmaus. It used to be called that, but is now called El-Qubeibeh. That alone was a major discovery.

The gospel story tells of Jesus meeting two disciples on the afternoon of the Resurrection while they were on their way home to Emmaus. It was described as a Sabbath day's journey, or roughly seven miles, from Jerusalem.

To my surprise, we did find Emmaus, and right next to it a road that passed right past the house. Another, much bigger road, the remains of an ancient Roman highway, lay about thirty feet away from the house, in the direction of the sea. Immediately off the spur running from the highway were the foundation and partial walls of a house dating back to the first century A.D. It is now incorporated into the back left-hand corner of the Franciscan church built on the site.

Entering the church, we could see the remains of the house in the back. I was impressed with the beautiful, well-preserved tile floor and a red cross painted on the ruins of the wall, the telltale mark by the earliest Christians that this site was authentically associated with Jesus' life.

The gospel story relating the incident of Jesus meeting the two disciples on their way to Emmaus is as follows:

When they were near the village to which they were going, He pretended to go farther. But they pressed Him, saying, "Stay with us, for it is getting towards evening and the day is already over." And He entered and stayed with them. While He reclined at table with them, He took bread, He recited the blessing, and He broke it and offered it to them. Then their eyes were opened and they recognized Him, but He disappeared from their sight. And one said to the other, "Was not our heart burning within us, when He spoke to us on the road and explained to us the scriptures?"

An interesting thing about that story is Jesus' attitude. He had not visited the apostles all day. They were still locked in the upper room of a house in Jerusalem where they were mourning Jesus' death. Now that He had visited with these two disciples and then disappeared, He realized they would run back to Jerusalem to tell the apostles that they had just seen Jesus. You can imagine them running the whole Sabbath day's journey, about seven miles, in their excitement to tell the apostles. However, Jesus, with His newfound glorified body, could now move with the speed of thought and appeared to the apostles first. What He said to them was significant for me. Passing through the solid stone wall, He greeted them: "Peace be with you. Receive the Holy Spirit. Whose sins you shall forgive, they are forgiven. Whose sins you shall retain, they are retained." I am sure this went right over the heads of the stunned apostles. If they had any reaction, it must have been "What is this all about?" Only later did it dawn on them the new power Jesus had bestowed on them: When apostate Christians repented and wanted to come back into the community, the apostles realized that Jesus had given them the power to reconcile people to God, to forgive their sins.

Understanding what had happened that night was important for me. I realized that when Jesus said the words "Receive the Holy Spirit" to the apostles, He was passing on to them the power to do something. The Jews believed that only God can forgive sins. This power Jesus was giving to the apostles certainly was not a personal privilege but a power that was to bring to many people the peace and joy of Jesus. The understanding of what those words meant came to them on the occasion of a rather severe persecution, when many Christians abandoned their faith rather than suffer torture or execution. When the persecution subsided, the people came back to the apostles, repentant and ashamed for what they had done. They asked if they could be received back into the community. The apostles were at a loss how to answer. They knew a person could not go back into the mother's womb. One of the early Fathers of the Church describes the episode: "We cannot baptize a second time, since they have already been reborn." After telling the people they would have to pray over the matter, the apostles were reminded of the night of the Resurrection. Saint James reminded them about the appearance of Jesus and what He had said to them: "Receive the Holy Spirit. Whose sins you shall forgive, they are forgiven them. Whose sins you shall retain, they are retained."

Maybe this was what Jesus was talking about. They agreed

unanimously, and then called back the penitents. After they made their heartfelt confession, the apostles gave them absolution and received them back into the community.

That was the beginning of reconciliation, or Confession, in the Church, long before the end of the first century. Later on the apostles were to extend Confession from apostasy to homicide and adultery, which was a scandal to the Christian community.

As time went by and the faith spread through the empire and the realities of life began more and more to impact Christian practice, bishops became more strict with regard to moral failings in the community. Public confession of notorious sin was required as well as public penance before the sinner would be granted absolution by the bishop and reconciliation with the community. For lesser sins, there were numerous ways of seeking forgiveness from God: almsgiving, personal penance, fasting, charitable works, private confession of sins to a priest.

There was a humorous side to our trip to Emmaus. As we were approaching the village, we spotted a group of people carting the carcass of a cow they had just killed. Other villagers were carrying chunks of the meat alongside the cart. Flies were all over the place. My father, who was a meat cutter and was always meticulously clean in handling meat products, lost his appetite for meat for the rest of the vacation. He did not complain about what we had just seen but slyly asked me, "Where's that place where we can get Saint Peter's fish?"

"The Sea of Galilee, Dad," I told him.

"I think we better go there next."

I just laughed. I knew what was on his mind. I told him Galilee was about a hundred miles away.

"That's not far. At least we'll know what we're eating when we see them catching the fish fresh out of the water."

We had supper in Capernaum that night and ate roasted fish, just as my father's namesake, Peter, used to eat many centuries ago.

AFTER OUR VISIT TO EMMAUS and before we drove to Galilee, my parents and I visited Mary and Martha and Lazarus' place, a beautiful restored compound of buildings on the presumably authentic site. Lazarus' tomb is also there. That was most impressive, though we did not stay long. We were eager to visit the other sites in Judea, and were inspired just knowing that Jesus once walked on these sites. My mother and father, with their beautifully simple faith, were probably more deeply moved than I was. I was more absorbed in analyzing everything and every place we visited to assure myself of its authenticity. "Find a reason for your faith" followed me everywhere. Even though I did not feel the warm piety my parents felt, I was benefiting from the powerful learning experience, which in itself was comforting.

After finishing our tour of Judea, we worked our way up through Samaria and into Galilee, which meant a lot to my father.

Jesus had promised to meet the apostles in Galilee, though He did not tell them where. Like the others after the Resurrection, this meeting turned out to be another shocking surprise. The apostles had been out on the lake fishing all night. They were tired and most likely irritable after having caught nothing. Then a voice called out to them from the shore: "Did you catch anything, young men?"

"No. We've been out here all night and did not catch a thing" was their reply. I suspect they expressed their frustration in language a bit more colorful.

"Throw your nets over the starboard side," the voice called out. There was probably a fog hovering over the lake, as they heard a voice but saw no one.

When they did as the voice instructed them, they caught a huge number of fish. John, who was always most alert, said to Peter, "It is the Lord."

When Peter heard that, he threw on his robe—they were fishing naked—and quickly made his way to shore. The others brought the boat to land.

Jesus was there standing by a charcoal fire, with a fish cooking on the coals.

"Bring some fish here," Jesus instructed them. While they were doing that, Jesus took Peter aside to talk with him privately.

"Simon, son of John, do you love me more than the others do?"

"Lord, you know that I love you."

"Feed my lambs."

Imagine two men talking like this.

Then again: "Simon, son of John, do you love me?"

"Lord, you know that I love you."

"Feed my sheep."

And then a third time, which must have hurt Peter deeply: "Simon, son of John, do you really love me?"

"Lord, you know all things. You know that I love you,"

Peter insisted with a heavy heart, realizing that he had denied Jesus three times and this was his penance.

"Feed my sheep."

Peter did not realize it then, but after he confessed his love for Jesus, Jesus was putting him in charge of the lambs, the sheep, and the whole flock. It was as if Jesus were saying, "I am about to leave. And I am placing all my disciples under your care. They are now your responsibility."

This touching exchange between Jesus and Peter meant a lot to me. It confirmed an issue I had been pondering for a long time. Yes, pondering, because this is an issue so long debated. On that spot, at that time, it became so clear to me. It became even more believable because it is John who is relating that Peter was placed in charge, and John had always contended with Peter for first place among the apostles. In fact, James and John's mother tried to get Jesus to promise them the first and second places when He set up the kingdom. So, John's relating the story says much. You can almost picture John eavesdropping when Jesus called Peter aside to talk to him, while the other apostles were supposed to be getting fish to put on the fire.

11

LIFE AFTER JESUS LEFT

*A*FTER THE EPISODES IN GALILEE, the apostles returned to Jerusalem where, shortly after, Jesus ascended from their midst into heaven. Before leaving, He told them He would not leave them orphans but would send the Holy Spirit, the Paraclete, the One who would be their strength and their comfort from then on. Of course, they did not understand most things that Jesus foretold to them until they actually happened.

After the Ascension of Jesus, the apostles and disciples—men and women, including Jesus' mother—spent time in prayer, wondering what God was expecting of them.

One day Peter, exercising for the first time his new position as leader of the group, addressed the community about the loss of Judas. Peter told them it was necessary for them to choose someone among the community to take the place of

Judas to complete the twelve whom Jesus had appointed as apostles, and one who could witness to the Resurrection of Jesus. The apostles nominated two men. The lot finally fell to Matthias, who from that time was listed as one of the apostles.

Shortly after this incident, on the Jewish feast of Pentecost, as the apostles met together, a loud sound came from out of nowhere and surrounded the house where they were staying. Immediately, what looked like tongues of fire appeared in the room and separated, coming to rest on the head of each apostle. Thereupon the apostles were filled with the Holy Spirit, whom Jesus had told them about, and they began to speak in various languages.

They wandered outside, still speaking in strange languages. Hearing the noise around the house, people had begun to gather, forming a large crowd. Since it was a festival season, there were many foreign Jews among them from all the surrounding countries. Some people laughed, thinking the apostles were drunk as they spoke strange languages; others were impressed because they could recognize that the apostles were speaking about God in their own languages.

Finally Peter stood up and motioned for silence. He said in a loud voice, "Men of Judea, and all you who live in Jerusalem, listen to what I have to say, and make no mistake about it, these men are not drunk. They are fulfilling the words of the prophet Isaiah, who foretold what is happening today." Peter then went on and spoke fearlessly about Jesus. When he finished, many believed and were converted that day.

From that day, despite arrests, threats, and punishments,

the apostles, with Peter always acting as spokesman, preached Jesus and His Resurrection throughout the city and at the temple itself, much to the anger of the high priest and his supporters, the Sadducees, who did not believe in life after death.

The community of believers grew each day, as the Church was becoming more firmly established and members met regularly to pray and care for one another. The community, mostly Jewish, worshiped at the temple daily and met at each other's homes for prayer and for the Eucharist, which they referred to as the breaking of bread.

At this point the community was well formed. Jesus apparently had taught them many practical things during the forty days following His Resurrection, because the apostles seemed to know precisely how to carry on Jesus' ministry on a day-to-day basis. Sharing with one another and caring for those in need in the community were highly organized activities. Many wealthy people turned over much of their fortune to the apostles to be distributed among the poor. Whenever any decisions had to be made, the matters were referred to Peter, who opened the meetings when the apostles gathered and acted as spokesman when statements were in order. Careful reading of the Acts of the Apostles shows Peter's prominence in the life of the earliest community not only in Judea but in Samaria and Caesarea, as well as in other cities, such as Lydda and Jaffa, in the north and along the coast. He was also the first to break the restriction on evangelizing the gentiles. After a vision and message from God, he was called to visit a prominent Roman centurion named Cornelius. After proclaiming Jesus as the Savior to Cornelius and his family and friends, Peter baptized them all. These were the first gentile converts.

The community grew rapidly, especially after a large group of priests and Pharisees were converted and baptized. The Church was well established in Judea and Galilee, and missionaries were already being sent out to Antioch, Damascus, and places even farther away.

12

DIFFICULT CHOICES

i WAS NOW BEGINNING TO FEEL comfortable with the scriptures and with the Jesus I was coming to understand in them. It was like feeling secure after laying the cornerstone of a building. The task at hand was to rebuild the rest of the structure. This was not as easy. In fact, it took many years to reconstruct what as a young person seemed so simple. All I can think of was that I had had a puzzle all nicely put together for me since childhood, then I dropped it and all the pieces scattered. Picking them up one by one and putting them all back in place was, I now realized, a most difficult task, and the tedious work of a whole lifetime. If I had to do it again, I would not have the energy, or the persistence, or the audacity. In fact, I was not merely putting pieces of a puzzle back together, but actually I was coming to a whole new understanding of faith and religion and spirituality and what they should mean in relation to life. It was as if I were becoming aware of an entirely different understanding of the message of Jesus and coming to a totally new understanding of spirituality based on what I had learned about Him, not only from studying the scriptures and theology but from my experience with life and what I had learned from the people I counseled and worked with in parishes, in schools, in prisons, in my own personal relationships throughout life.

My first major shock was tied up with the depression that I was experiencing during my seminary days. I had always wanted to be a saint. I was inspired by the saints' total dedication to Jesus, by their serene and intimate relationship with God in their contemplative prayer life. I wanted that more than anything. Being a monk, I knew sainthood was attainable. It was the whole purpose of monastic life to attain intimacy with God in prayer and contemplation. The key to growth in contemplation is discipline, discipline of the senses, discipline in dedication to daily prayer and meditation, discipline of the emotions so we can focus our energies on the spiritual life. The most difficult part of trying to be holy is ridding ourselves of unhealthy sinful tendencies that are so much a part of being human. Getting to know myself was the starting line. Getting to know myself meant learning what had to be changed, sublimated, or rooted out of my personality.

As I had boundless energy, I set up my battle lines on many different fronts. I knew quite well my personal weaknesses, my tendencies, and what I had to do to set out on the road to becoming a saint.

In seminary, we rose at six o'clock each morning, except on Saturday and Sunday, when we could sleep till seven. I woke up even earlier and spent time alone taking a walk and spending quiet time with God. At Mass and prayer, I would not allow distractions to interfere with my meditations. As I was prone to seek my comfort, I slept on boards under my sheets, rather than a mattress, and took only cold showers to discipline my natural tendencies as a teenager, trying to deal with sexual feelings. We studied for three hours each day. I sat erect and disciplined my thoughts so I could develop better powers of concentration. To my surprise, I did not find these things difficult. After a while, they became second nature. I did miss not being able to go out with girls. That was painful and difficult to cope with, especially since there were some girls I knew who liked me and hoped I would not stay in the seminary. I liked them as well. But my desire to be a saint overrode all these needs, and what seemed impossible became only extremely difficult, a constant distraction.

With the onset of the depression that was to hold me in its terrifying grip for almost twelve years, I lost the vast energy that made all the discipline possible. I could not maintain the strict regimen I had imposed on myself. Praying became impossible. I had the sad feeling that God did not want to be close to me anymore. Why? Was I a terrible sinner? Had I done something evil? Was I a disappointment to God? Maybe God did not want me to be a priest. Maybe I was not supposed to be here.

The Carmelite Order that I belonged to as a postulant was dedicated to prayer and contemplation. There were all kinds of books in the novitiate library that I had spotted when I went to visit my spiritual director, Father John Haffert. The man was a saint. He knew me quite well, and as ascetic and

saintly as he was, I knew he enjoyed directing me. Whenever
he saw me he would smile, as if he were pleased that I was so
interested in the spiritual life even though I was only sixteen
years old. He kindly let me borrow the mystical theology
books that described the various stages of the spiritual life. He
showed me sections I might find helpful: sections on the Dark
Night of the Senses and the Illuminative Way, phases of
growth along the way of the contemplative life. I found peace
in reading these manuals, though when one of the other
priests saw me reading them, he told me they were too deep
for me, that they were for theologians. "But I understand
them, and they help me a lot," I told him. I don't think he believed me, but he said no more.

One particular book, *The Spiritual Life,* by Father Adolphe
Tanquerey, was most important in helping me to understand
that the frightening feeling that God was disappointed with
me was off the mark. This phenomenon I was experiencing
was a stage in the natural development of the spiritual life.
The tender feeling of God's presence was a gift God gives us
in the beginning. Then, as our attachment to Him becomes
stronger and more secure, He leads us into a deeper relationship, where we begin to live by faith, not by nice feelings.
However, this phase is painful because the soul feels as if God
has abandoned it. That is why it is called the Dark Night of
the Senses. If a person remains faithful to God during that
trying period, then God infuses beautiful thoughts into the
person's soul, giving meaning and understanding to things
that previously were incomprehensible. That phase is called
the Illuminative Way because it is filled with many enlightening insights. That made so much sense to me and explained

why I was beginning to see so many things in my life that I did not understand before, such as the fact that some people who had very evil ways still were able to do many good and heroic things in their lives. Before, I always looked on people as either good or bad. Now I was beginning to see that there is bad even in the best of us and good even in the worst of us, and that God is working differently in each person's life, which explains why everyone grows differently and at a different pace. It helped me to be more humble and less judgmental of people I had previously considered bad, even of other seminarians who did not seem to have an enthusiasm for the spiritual life and seemed interested in other things. It helped me to see myself as becoming pharisaical in my attitudes toward others, which could totally destroy my whole spiritual life if I did not overcome it.

Some of the things written in these spiritual manuals, however, I found to be not workable in real life, though the paths they proposed were what people of all denominations taught—for example, a life of holiness must be based on the perfect observance of all the commandments and spiritual counsels, and on living a saintly life. I tried that and had been successful at it for a while, but then found out that it is impossible to be perfectly observant of all the ideals of religion or even to avoid all sin. Doing so entails fighting a thousand different battles on a thousand different fronts. Human nature is beset by strong tendencies and driven by so many conflicting feelings that to attempt to do everything perfectly can make a person a nervous wreck and even lead to a nervous breakdown. I was learning to be humble and realize I was just like everyone else, struggling to be good, but still very human, frail, weak—in short, a sinner. I was beginning to learn humility for the first time in my life, a genuine humility that came from shame and an honest realization of my weaknesses.

A very comforting and profound book, I think its name was *The Love of God,* by an English priest named Father Frederick Faber, helped me to understand that God is not shocked by our weaknesses. He expects it because He never intended to make us perfect. And it is our sinfulness, which comes from our human weakness, that entitles us to God's mercy and compassion. That meant so much to me and more than anything helped me to realize that God still loved me. For the next few years I kept analyzing what would be a sensible approach to a life of holiness or a sensible path to spiritual growth. In reading the gospels and meditating on Jesus' teachings, I noticed Jesus kept talking about everything happening in due time, in due season. Things grow and mature in due time, in their own season; everything in its own time. There is a vast understanding of human nature in what Jesus says. One of the things that I began to understand is that human beings are not all made the same, nor does God expect the same thing from everyone all at once. Jesus' casual acceptance of the apostles' idiosyncrasies and failings is a good example of that. Another powerful example is the calm way in which Jesus accepts everyone where they are at and does not pressure people to change their lives all at once. It is interesting that nowhere in the gospels do you see Jesus criticizing anybody, other than the scribes and Pharisees, because of their hypocrisy. The message seemed to me to be loud and clear: Everyone is different, designed differently by God, and each has a different function to perform in God's plan, so the growth process and training of each person are different depending on what God has planned for that person to accomplish in life.

As a result, each person's spirituality is custom-designed and the training process is tailor-made to fit what God intends for that person to accomplish.

So often we expect people to be where we are in the spiritual life, and we pressure them to be what we think they should be and where we think they should be spiritually. Now I realize that is arrogant; we have no idea what God is trying to accomplish in a person's life and what special training God is putting that person through so he or she can be properly prepared for some special work. For us to pressure people to be what we want them to be can interfere with what the Holy Spirit may be trying to accomplish with them.

This interference is most notable in people who continually harass others to accept salvation, which would have been part of my personality. Even Jesus was not compulsive in pushing people into salvation. He offered it. If they wanted it, wonderful. If they didn't want it, then that was their choice. In time, perhaps they would be ready and then they would accept it. Saint Francis, as saintly as he was, taught that we preach Jesus by the lives we live and that we should use words only when absolutely necessary. People followed Jesus after Francis' example not because he was a great preacher, but because they saw Jesus living in him and in the way he lived his own life.

Now two or three pieces of the puzzle finally fit into place. I saw that God was not angry with me, still loved me, and understood my weaknesses, which drew from Him His compassionate mercy. I now understood my depression as part of the spiritual growth process as God was leading me into a deeper relationship with Himself and sharing new insights, which were very clear and thrilling, but baffling to me because they were different. I was learning things about God that were not part of what I had been taught about Him, and it was all new to me. Growing spiritually meant getting to know God more deeply. Growth means change. Change is always frightening. Change for teenagers is always frightening because so much is unfamiliar and fraught with terrifying dangers of all sorts. Being far from home and family and living with strangers forced me to face all the interior turmoil by myself. Added to that were these changing ideas about God. Getting to know God more deeply meant my ideas about God were different from what I had been taught as a child. Seeing God differently was comforting, but also unfamiliar territory. For a long while it was confusing and frightening for me, because there was no way of telling which understanding of God was right. Each day brought to light new facets of God, as if God Himself were teaching me, but it was all new and different. I was happy, but my happiness was tinged with sadness because I was moving away from what I was familiar with from childhood. It was like telling a child there is no Santa Claus, which is a very distressing experience. A changing concept of God is unsettling, and though my changing ideas were positive and comforting, there was a measure of insecurity, since they were making me feel even more different from others. Was it good for me to learn what I was learning, or was it making me an oddity?

I felt that what I was learning was good and that it might

be a help later on when I was dealing with people who were going through difficult times in their own lives. I also needed to know that God was compassionate and understanding. In spite of my confusion, I knew I had to continue on the road I was now traveling.

13

JOURNEY ALONG
A NEW ROAD

*a*s I BECAME AWARE that my understanding of God was changing, I also noticed that my attitude toward many other things was changing. Before, my image of God was tightly defined within human parameters. He would act, I thought, the way a good human being would act, with the same human responses: happy, sad, angry, disappointed, just, and judgmental. That idea was now changing. God was too big to be human. His reaction patterns, as reflected in Jesus' life, were radically different from the reaction patterns of humans. I began to realize the meaning of the verses in scripture saying that God's thoughts and His ways are far beyond our thoughts and our ways. He sees into the heart of each of us when He judges. We judge by what we see on the surface of people's lives. He was not judgmental in the harsh way we are. Jesus could see into people's hearts and understand their pain, and could find reason to show pity. When Jesus saw a prostitute,

He did not see a sinner. He saw a woman in deep pain, scarred from childhood by the meanness and cruelty of others, but within possessing vast untapped goodness and tenderness. When He saw a despised tax collector, He did not see a crook, a despised public sinner. He saw a man struggling to support a family, with skills too limited to earn a living in a trade or private undertaking, but a man whose poor self-image could appreciate a kindness done to him and a man who could be a dedicated disciple if he was shown the way.

What was remarkable about Jesus—and Jesus was the living reflection of God—was that He could pass over the shabby, crude exterior in people's lives and see, deep within, their potential for goodness. Reflecting back to them the goodness He saw in them changed their own image of themselves and inspired them to holiness—not all at once, perhaps, but as the grace of God nurtured them.

The image of God in my mind was expanding in a way that made it difficult for me to envision God the way I used to. God was so far above all that was human, so different from the way humans think and feel and judge, that in a way it was becoming hard to relate to Him. He was not a male or a female. He had no body. How do you relate to someone you cannot see or even fashion in your imagination? Clinging to Jesus was my only connection with God. What I saw of God reflected in Jesus was beauty and goodness and infinite compassion. Harsh justice was never a part of Jesus, so I could not see harsh justice as a trait of His heavenly Father who is Eternal Love. Harsh justice I now saw as a human trait, tied in with our petty craving for retribution and revenge. That kind of attitude now appeared unworthy of God.

My daily meditations in the monastery were, as always, focused on Jesus, even though, because of my depression and stress, it was still difficult for me to concentrate. One of our theology courses was called patrology. It was an intensive course on the writings of the early Fathers of the Church. These men lived in the time of the apostles and shortly thereafter. They were prodigious writers; many had been Greek or Roman or African philosophers or literary figures before they became Christians.

After their conversion they continued writing, but now their subject matter was the Christian message and what the apostles were teaching the Christian communities about Jesus and His Good News of salvation. The witness of the Fathers of the Church is invaluable because they reflect ideas and practices the apostles had learned from Jesus and were passing on to their disciples. Many of those ideas and practices were not written into the gospels or the apostles' letters, but still reflected what Jesus taught. One of these writings, the Didache, or the Teachings of the Twelve Apostles, was a most important handbook for the earliest Christian communities. In fact, at one point in the first century it was incorporated into the canon of the New Testament. Though it was later dropped, it is still looked on as reflecting the mind of the apostles. This book contains instructions as to how to go about living the Christian life on a daily basis and how certain sacraments are to be performed. One part provides instructions on Baptism. When preparing for Baptism, for example, the priest should fast the day before the convert is to be baptized. The person or persons to be baptized should also fast.

When performing Baptism, the priest should use living water, which means running water, as from a stream or a nearby brook. The ones to be baptized should go down into the water. If there is no running water, then any kind of water may be used. If there is only a small amount of water, the priest is to pour it over the person's head while saying, "I baptize you in the name of the Father, and of the Son, and of the Holy Spirit." If there is a very large crowd and no ready supply of water, the priest is to sprinkle with water the crowd that is to be baptized, saying the same words as before. I was surprised at the casual flexibility of the apostles in the performance of the rite. Obviously they were more concerned with the meaning of baptism than with the mechanics of the rite itself. The book also provides detailed instructions for celebrating the Eucharist. The Didache fascinated me because most probably it was written while some of the apostles were still alive or only recently deceased. Dated to around the end of the first century, it certainly reflects the apostles' teaching.

Once I was introduced to the Fathers of the Church, they became an important part of my entire life. I still read them every day in some form or other. They have been invaluable in my effort to evaluate not only my own beliefs but the teachings and practices in the Church as well, and also the beliefs and practices of other denominations. There are hundreds of volumes of these writings, and familiarity with them gives the reader a good idea of how faithful various churches have remained to the beliefs and practices of the Christian communities taught by the apostles themselves.

One facet of the early evangelizing by the apostles that impressed me deeply was its simplicity. The apostles did not evangelize by teaching scripture to Roman, Greek, or other gentile peoples. Nor did they teach theology or use theological terminology when speaking with their disciples, though their ideas contained solid theological content. Instead, they shared their memories of Jesus and all that Jesus had taught them. They shared with their converts their own relationship with Jesus, so that the converts' religion was intimacy with Jesus, not dedication to a church. Jesus was their religion. He was their Lord and Savior. The Church was the medium of Jesus' message, and although the Church was the body of Christ sharing Jesus' life, which they received in Baptism, it was Jesus who was the focus of religion, not the community.

What was impressive about the early Christians was their close-knit relationships. No one was a stranger. People became members of a family when they entered the community, bonded as brothers and sisters. They still had their rivalries and their jealousies, and pettiness, just as in any family, but the family bond was there, sensitizing them to one another's needs and problems. Their religious services were held on Sunday evenings. Sunday was the day made sacred by the Lord's Resurrection, so it became the common practice for the Christians to gather on that day. Besides, Jewish Christians still attended synagogue services on the Sabbath; there was no real break with the Jewish community until later. Having Christian services on Sunday prevented a conflict for Jewish Christians. It was interesting to see how the Christians in widely separated communities were following pretty much the same practices and customs. Uniformity was already developing in the communities established by the apostles, though as they wandered farther away into different countries, their simple ritual for the breaking of bread, the

Eucharist, took on slight variations influenced by the culture of the people. Thomas eventually passed through Syria and then worked his way east. He seems to have finally settled in India, where he established a community of Christians that has lasted till this day. Their way of celebrating the Eucharist was influenced by the various people he evangelized. An ancient Eucharistic rite still exists in the Church in India, along with their own jealously guarded version of Church law that allows optional celibacy among the priests.

Many of the converts in the early Church were among the lower classes in society. A considerable number of highly educated people accepted Jesus' message as well, as is shown by the intellectual caliber of the Fathers of the Church. If some of the Christians were wealthy, it was not because of noble birth, but most probably because they were successful merchants.

Early on, the apostles realized that they could not stay in the communities they established. If they were to spread the gospel to others, they had to keep moving. Soon they had to make provisions for others to guide the communities they established. After training a trustworthy man, the apostle would pray over the man, laying hands on him and calling down the Holy Spirit upon him, thus sharing the authority and power Jesus had given to the apostles. Power and authority were passed on through this laying on of hands and calling down the Holy Spirit. It was Jesus' way of continuing His mission to all future generations. In every community where the apostles went they did the same thing, appointed and ordained bishops to guide and govern the community in their place.

The Fathers of the Church paint vivid portraits of the place of these bishops in the early Church. Timothy and Titus were among the first to be appointed and ordained personally by Saint Paul. As far back as the end of the first century, it is clear that these bishops were key persons in the Church. Saint Ignatius of Antioch writes extensively about the place of the bishop in the community.

Knowing he would soon be headed for Rome for his martyrdom, Ignatius wrote letters of appreciation and guidance to the various churches that sent delegates to meet with him at Smyrna, where the ship he was on wintered. While there this venerable old man witnessed not only the remarkable expressions of love and deep faith among the Christians, but also unseemly conflicts and personality clashes in the communities and, on occasion, unjustified rancor against one of their bishops.

Ignatius wrote to remind them to be loyal to their bishops. Having been ordained by the apostles, the bishops share the authority given to the apostles by Jesus, and just like the apostles, they stand in the place of God, just as the priests and deacons stand in the place of Jesus.

At the time, some of the more excitable among the people had left the community and had gone off and started their own communities. Ignatius warned them that no Christians who reject their bishop can be pleasing to Christ and that no sacrifice offered by these people would be pleasing to God. In walking away from their bishop, they walk away from Jesus, and no one should dare attempt to celebrate the Eucharist without the bishop's presence. In doing such a thing, how could they be pleasing to God? Loyalty to bishops was a common theme among the early Fathers of the Church, because many undisciplined Christians were prone to bitter internal squabbles. Such squabbles so divided members that factions would break with the communities and start their own churches, thus fracturing the Church, which, as Saint Paul had taught them, is the body of Christ. These internal conflicts haunted Paul, especially while he was away on missionary journeys, and occasioned more than one of his passionate letters, in which he warned the hotheads not to tear apart the Church by their incessant bickering, or they would have to answer to God for the damage they were causing to the body of Christ.

My filtering of what I was reading about the early Church was rewarding but also disturbing. Bishops back then were real leaders, unafraid of controversy and highly intelligent defenders of the faith passed on to them from the apostles. They were men of passionate faith, willing to sacrifice themselves totally, even to their death, if need be, to defend their faith. As I was learning more and more about Church life today, I did not see very many bishops of that caliber. I saw them more as pious men who were rewarded for their faithful service—company men, as they would be called in industry. It was difficult to respect them; they seemed more concerned about their political future than about the priests or people under their care.

It was rare to hear a spiritually inspiring sermon or one of a theological nature, discussing dangerous moral or unchristian ideas circulating among the Christian community. Bishops might mention them superficially if there was a current public issue, but they did not provide the people with solid rational or theological arguments explaining what should be a thinking Christian's understanding of such issues. I will never forget the night after a particular bishop was made archbishop; the man was being interviewed on television and was asked about his attitude toward abortion. His answer was "I am naturally opposed to abortion because it is contrary to the teachings of the Catholic Church." I cringed. What a sad reason for a religious leader to be for or against any issue. My first reaction was, "Can't this man do his own thinking? If he is going to be the official teacher of his archdiocese, he is going to be a sorry shepherd." A religious leader should be able to analyze an issue and determine why a particular moral stance is either good or bad based on the merits of the issue itself. Jesus gave us the basis for making moral judgments. His principle was "The Sabbath was made for man, not man for the Sabbath." The law was made for man, not man for the law. The basis for all law has to be not only the good of the individual but also the ultimate good of the community and society in general.

At the time the archbishop made his comments about the abortion issue, I had just been reading about the beginning of communism in Russia. In the beginning, the Communists encouraged abortion, but after the first generation they realized it was a horrible mistake, because the country was having a severe shortage of skilled labor, of scientists and engineers, which was jeopardizing their national security. They decided that abortion was rapidly becoming a cause for national concern. The Communists were not religious people. They were crass pragmatists. Within a short time they passed a law subsidizing married couples to have children. Concern for hu-

man life was not their interest. The decision was purely political. The archbishop's comment made me sad because it
seemed to be politically motivated. Not that the good man
was not interested in human life. I know he was, and he
turned out to be a caring bishop, but the fact that he did not
express his own well-reasoned principles concerning such a
critical issue in our nation depressed me. He could have at
least said, "I am opposed to abortion because it is the destruction of a human life." That would have revealed a much
stronger person who did his own thinking and could make a
strong statement on a moral issue.

At the same time of the interview with the archbishop,
there was an interview with the leading proponent of abortion
in England. When asked if he believed that a baby growing in
its mother's womb was a human being, he answered without
hesitation, "You cannot deny that it is a human life; I admit
that it is human. But there are reasons, out of compassion,
that sometimes justify taking the life of an unborn baby." The
discussion continued from there. At least he did not just say,
"I am in favor of abortion because all my friends are in favor
of abortion."

I learned much from reading the Fathers of the Church,
and still learn much, old as I am, because they reflect for me
the ideas and witness of strong, highly intelligent religious
leaders, as well as a vibrant Christianity filled with the power
and energy that still received its force from its proximity to
Jesus' Resurrection. His followers were, for the most part,
fired with a zeal for their faith that inspired them to total
commitment, even to martyrdom if the chance arose. We see
that zeal for the faith today occasionally in individuals rather

than in a whole community, and I guess that is the definition of a modern-day saint, a person who is on fire with the love of Jesus, and never lets that fire grow cold, and whose witness is all the more beautiful because it is so rare.

What was fascinating in my studying the Fathers of the Church and the life of the early Christians was that, as close as they were to the time of Jesus, their interest in religion was, for the most part, driven by a need to understand and define who Jesus really was and what He was. Was He really God, or was He a kind of divinized human? Was His body a real human body, or was it a phantom body? Was He just a God living in human flesh, or was He both God and a human being? For two hundred years they grappled with those problems. And the controversies were so hotly debated that even Roman emperors and the Roman army became involved. This two-hundred-year theological conflict created a drama that has all the human interest material for a gripping three-hour movie or a television series.

Part of the controversy involved the relationship between Jesus and His mother. Since her Son was God, could she be called the Mother of God? The Christian people already referred to Mary as the Mother of God, but some powerful clergy were reluctant to allow the use of such a title. A debate over that issue lasted for years. After much bitter controversy, the issue was finally resolved at the Council of Ephesus in A.D. 431, when it was decided that a mother gives birth not just to a body but to a person, and since Jesus was a divine person, Mary could reasonably be referred to as the Mother of God, the Theotokos, the God-bearer. It was understood that Mary was not the origin of Jesus' divinity. The night of that decision, the people of Ephesus went wild with celebration, parading through the streets in a huge torchlight procession. It is easy to understand the enthusiasm of the Ephesians for Mary's special title. Ephesus had been the home of Jesus' mother while she was under the care of Saint John the Apostle. In fact, there still exists a house there where Mary lived, a place also highly venerated by Muslims in the community and a place of pilgrimage. It is the site where a tradition tells that after Mary died, she was assumed into heaven even while her body was being guarded through the night. It was from Ephesus that the belief in the assumption of Mary spread throughout the Church.

The course in patrology was invaluable for my understanding of the nature of Jesus and His relationship with the other Persons of the Holy Trinity, as well as defining precisely his role as Savior and as Mediator with the Father and as Head of the Mystical Body. What surprised me was how extensively the Fathers of the Church wrote about Mary, Jesus' mother. I wondered how this interest in Mary began and what occasioned it, because there is not a large amount of material about her in the gospels or in the Acts of the Apostles. Only later on did I find out that the Christian community's veneration of Mary started very early. At Nazareth there is a house, excavated in the nineteenth century, that seems to have been the place where Mary lived before she married Joseph. On one of the walls is a red cross, identifying the site as authentically associated with Jesus' life. Adjacent to this house and attached to it is a shrine, a small room, with these words inscribed on a wall: "This shrine has been built and dedicated to Mary, the Mother of Jesus, by her family and friends." Currently there is a large modern church, the Church of the Annunciation, constructed over this modest ancient structure, located in a spacious vault beneath the church, convenient for the public to spend time meditating on the mystery that took place there so many centuries ago.

The first church in Nazareth is a church-synagogue, built near the grotto dedicated to Mary, evidencing the existence of a very early Jewish Christian community living in Nazareth. The fact that they had their own public structure indicates a strong and well-established community.

It did make sense to me that the earliest Christian community would be close to Mary after Jesus left. She was the closest living bond with Jesus and, as His mother, was held in high esteem by the original community. She was the only one who could satisfy the interest and curiosity of His many followers who wanted to know more about Him, especially the details of His childhood and early years. When the young community gathered for prayer and the breaking of bread, she was always part of it. She was an intimate part of everything that happened in the life of the apostles and helped them to better understand her Son. Saint Luke's gospel must have been written after many interviews with Mary. She is the only one who could have given him the intimate details of her life that he describes in his gospel.

The Fathers indicate that Mary was the first one to see Jesus after His Resurrection, as He came to assure her that He was still alive. The Acts of the Apostles mentions Mary's presence with them after the Ascension and that she was with them continually in prayer. Mary seems to have been the heart of the young community and a source of strength and encouragement to them. When John left Jerusalem and went to Ephesus, Mary accompanied him, and she remained with him until God took her home. I wondered if the reason John speaks in such glorious terms about the mother of the Savior in the Book of Revelation was because while she was with him for so many years, he contemplated the beauty of her life and the mystical place she occupied in the divine drama of our redemption. Was she the woman clothed with the sun, crowned with a diadem of twelve stars, and with the moon under her feet whom John describes in Revelation, and the woman whose Son Satan tried so hard to destroy and whose other children, the family of her Son's disciples, he was determined to harm? Was John's idea of Mary transformed into a glorious being after she died, separated by God from the rest of humanity and with almost a cosmic role to play in God's vast universal kingdom? John knew Jesus had placed him, John, in the role of son and placed her in the role of his mother. Was John beginning to see Mary, especially after her death, not just as *his* mother but as the mother of *all* the children born into Jesus by baptism, and as such a serious threat to Satan? It seems so, as later on John refers to all of the woman's children whom Satan was trying to destroy.

What I was learning from the Fathers of the Church was important to me because these were issues I had to grapple with. I believed in the divinity of Jesus. I believed Jesus was also human. The thought of God becoming a creature and becoming part of our human existence was a difficult issue to struggle with. Our relationship with Mary was also an issue. My father and mother were always dedicated to the Blessed Mother, and as a child I was taught to pray to Mary and ask her protection, and ask that she pray to Jesus for me. Both my parents prayed the rosary every day. I could not understand why the rosary should be important. I prayed to the Blessed Mother and had a devotion to her as Jesus' mother, but I had to try to understand the many issues involved in Mary's relationship with each Person of the Trinity, since in scripture it is mentioned but not clearly defined. God the Father sent the archangel Gabriel to propose to Mary. He was gracious in asking her consent out of respect for her free will. The archangel said she would have the Child by the overshadowing of the Holy Spirit and that the Holy One born of her would be the Son of God. Nowhere in scripture is anyone else depicted as having such an intimate relationship with the three Persons of the Trinity. That impressed me, though it was late in life that I came to realize the full force of what that meant, and the stupendous honor for her to work so closely with each Person of the Trinity. It is humbling for me to realize that I still have so much to learn about my faith. Where have I been in my spiritual travels?

It took a Jewish person, my agent and dear friend Peter Ginsberg, to make me realize that there was something out of focus in my portrait of Jesus in my book *Joshua*.

One day he told me he would like me to do another Joshua manuscript. I was shocked, as I had been told that Joshua as a series had run its course. I asked why he would like me to do another Joshua.

"Because I would like you to include His mother this time."

"Peter, you are Jewish. Why would you suggest something like this?"

"I just came back from Turkey. There is a city there, Ephesus, where Jesus' mother lived when she was under the care of John the Apostle. The house where she lived is still there. When I walked across the threshold, I was deeply moved, and thought about it, and realized that Mary was always by Jesus' side and a part of His ministry, and in none of your Joshua books do you include her. That is why I would like you to write another Joshua manuscript, and this time include His mother in His ministry."

I have to admit I was deeply moved by what he said but did not know how I could write a manuscript including Jesus' mother and make it believable. In fact, one of the biggest reasons why I would not even allow myself to entertain the thought was because seeing Mary involved in Jesus' ministry would not be acceptable to my many Protestant readers. It would look like I was proselytizing. I did not even know how I could handle the subject in a novel. It was not until our government began putting so many Arab people in detention centers that I found a way to introduce Mary. Muslims have a deep devotion to the mother of Jesus. It would make sense and would be understandable to involve her in the lives of decent Muslim people hurting over the cruelty and injustice done to them by their own terrorist husbands sending their sons to their deaths as suicide bombers, as well as the meanness and injustice on the part of "patriotic" Christians. It would be a beautiful image of the mutual love of Jesus and His mother to portray Mary as an important part of Jesus' ministry to bring peace to the troubled Middle East in the context of a novel.

Since then I have done much thinking about Mary and

her role in our salvation. I had spent my whole life trying to make sense out of Jesus and to understand His message, and I had a good sense of Mary's role in our redemption, but now I had to look more deeply into that role and her place in our lives.

What is Mary's relationship with the Church and with individual Christians? That was a question I had to resolve for myself. Is she like a special saint, or is Mary, as Jesus' mother, something more than a saint? These were not easy issues, and there were whole sections of theology dealing with Mary and her place in the story of salvation. Fortunately, my seminary training gave me the background and resources to research these important aspects of theology. I don't know what I would have done if I had not had such easy access to all this material. I can understand why so few people ever make the effort to understand their faith, as doing so can be quite impossible if there is no easy access to the material necessary for study.

Since the Second Vatican Council in the 1960s, devotion to Jesus' mother has gone through a very thorough reevaluation. In the past many devout Catholics prayed to Mary; indeed, some seemed to have placed more emphasis on her than on her Son. Yet when you talked to these people, they would always say that they looked on Jesus as their God, but they felt close to Mary because they felt she was a mother and could understand their problems, especially problems with their children. And Mary did have problems with her Child; He was a constant source of worry and concern. The Council wisely steered a prudent course concerning devotion to Jesus' mother. While upholding the many theologically solid aspects of Mary's relationship with Jesus and the Church and individual Christians, it encouraged a more prudent approach to private devotion to Mary, as some pious devotees of Mary seemed to have depended more on Mary than on Jesus for their salvation.

14

UNANSWERED QUESTIONS

i ALWAYS LOOKED TO THE EARLY documents to find the roots of what Christians should believe, because scripture does not contain everything that Jesus said and did, as Saint John writes at the end of his gospel. The early Fathers of the Church, reflecting what the apostles had taught the first Christians, are a credible witness to the beliefs as well as the lifestyle and practices of the early Christian communities. When it came to Mary, however, I was limited in what I could find. The early Fathers did believe in the virgin birth and the unsullied life of Mary, the complete sanctity of her life as witnessed by the greeting of the angel at the annunciation: "Hail, full of grace! The Lord is with you. Blessed are you among women." Also from earliest days, the Christians believed that Mary, like Enoch, Elias, and Moses, was taken up into heaven. A number of the Fathers, including Timothy of Jerusalem, John the Theologian, Gregory of Tours, Theoteknos of Livias, and John Damascene, refer not to Mary's death but to her *dormition,* her sleep, and then her body being taken up into heaven.

Her continued presence and intimacy with the early Christians showed the respect in which she was held. There is no stronger witness than the most honored position in which God Himself placed her by choosing her to be the mother of His Son. What greater honor could be bestowed on a mere human?

The one theological idea that impressed me was that the Church is, as Saint Paul writes, "the body of Christ." Jesus is the head; we are the members. If Mary is the mother of Jesus, and Jesus shares His life with us through baptism, then, by extension, she is our mother too. Then, too, she consented to bring our Savior into the world, for which I had to feel gratitude.

But that still did not help me decide that she should be part of my prayer life in any significant way. Then I asked myself: If I lived in Jesus' day, and I went to visit Him, and His mother was present, how would I treat her? Obviously with the greatest respect, because of my love for Him. If I got to know her as a person, I would feel honored that she was my friend, and then I would probably feel very comfortable asking her to ask her Son when I needed help, knowing that she'd have a better chance than I would, as she did at the wedding party at Cana.

Finally, it did make good theological sense for me to feel comfortable developing a warm relationship with Jesus' mother. It was surprising how comforting such a relationship can be in most troubled times. I now understood why my mother and father felt so close to the Blessed Mother or, as my godchild Peter calls her, "Mother Mary."

Another question I had that was a cause of great concern was the position of the pope. My first question was a simple one. Why was he called "pope"? What does that mean? All I had to do was look that up in an encyclopedia, which I did. The word "pope" is taken from the Latin word *papa* (meaning "father") and was used by all bishops in the early Western Church. In the early Eastern Church, the term was used when referring to priests. The patriarch of Alexandria is always called "pope." Solving that problem was simple enough. Currently, in the Western Church, the title is used only when referring to the Bishop of Rome.

In resolving the other issues concerning the Bishop of Rome, the task was not so easy. I searched for many years. The search was confusing, as I found myself reading material by others who did not have a solid foundation in ancient church history or who slanted material in a negative way. When I did my own research, I got an entirely different understanding. I finally found information that was helpful in the writings of Saint Irenaeus. Saint Irenaeus was a student or disciple of Saint Polycarp. Polycarp was born around A.D. 69 and was one of the earliest Fathers of the Church, having been a disciple of Saint John the Apostle and a direct witness to the teachings of the apostles. He ordained Irenaeus to the priesthood and sent him as a missionary to Gaul in northern Europe, where he spent most of his time fighting strange ideas being circulated about Jesus and Christian teachings. Saint Irenaeus was a witness to authentic teachings received from the apostles and passed on through the Church since earliest times.

Much of Irenaeus' writings dealt with popular distortions of Jesus' teachings and in countering the belief that the end of the world was imminent. He also spelled out very clearly where the authentic teachings of Jesus were to be found. "It is," he wrote in the second chapter of the Third Book, "Adversus Haereses,"

> within the power of all, therefore, in every Church, who may wish to see the truth, contemplate clearly the tradition of the apostles manifested throughout the whole world, and we are in a position to list those who were by the apostles instituted bishops in the Churches, and to [demonstrate] the succession of these men in our own times. . . . However, since it would be tedious . . . to track the succession of all the Churches, we do put to confusion all those who, in whatever manner, whether by an evil self-pleasing, by vainglory, or by blindness and perverse opinion, assemble in unauthorized meetings, [we do this, I say] by indicating that tradition derived from the apostles, of the very great, the very ancient, and universally known Church founded and organized at Rome by the two most glorious apostles, Peter and Paul; as also [by pointing out] the faith preached to men, which comes down to our time by means of the succession of bishops. For it is a matter of necessity that every Church should agree with this Church, on account of its preeminent authority.

Irenaeus then went on to list the successors of Peter as Bishop of Rome: Linus, Cletus, Clement (who wrote to the Church at Corinth encouraging them to make peace with their bishop and to be faithful to the traditions that had been passed on to them), Evaristus, Sixtus, Telephorus, Hyginus, Pius, Anicetus, Soter, and Eleutherius, who was Bishop of Rome in Irenaeus' time. Eleutherius was the one who upset Irenaeus because he was so reluctant to take a strong stand against the spread of some dangerous ideas.

Reading this from such a prominent and respected spiritual "grandson" of John the Evangelist, I realized I had finally found authentic testimony not only about Peter being in Rome but about the necessity of other churches being in tune with Rome as the guardian of the authentic traditions handed down from the apostles. This was important to me because I had been told so often by friends not of my faith that there was no evidence of Peter even having been in Rome; their words made me wonder what was right and what was wrong. It also pointed out that the Bishop of Rome had a clear responsibility to monitor what was happening in the other churches, as shown by Saint Clement's exhorting the Church at Corinth to make peace among themselves and with their bishop. In his letter, Clement showed a gentle use of authority that is rare among Church officials. So many of them like to make their authority felt. Yet Clement knew it was his responsibility to try to heal the wounds among the sheep in that distant part of the flock. The Bishop of Rome may not have been aware of his power yet, but he was sensitive to his responsibility for even distant members of Jesus' flock.

It was not easy for me to keep digging and digging for a "reason for my faith." The more I learned, the heavier became the burden to understand all the complexities that developed in the kingdom of heaven on earth, this beautiful "pearl of great price" Jesus talked about. I was beginning to see cropping up a dark side to the kingdom, a side that was painful, a very human tendency to lose sight of Jesus in the fierce battles to define what Christians should believe and the meanness toward others who saw things differently. It was painful to see the intolerance and the pettiness among highly intelligent bishops and theologians, and their unwillingness to be gracious toward those with different views. And this did not end. It stayed with the Church all through its history. Sometimes the Church even condemned to death those convicted of heresy and had them burned at the stake. In their dedication to dogma, they lost total sight of the gentle, forgiving Jesus they were supposed to be representing. Instead, they did more damage to the name of Jesus and to people's faith than heretics did with all their strange theological ideas. Continuing the search became more and more painful for me, as I had to see things that I wished I did not have to think about. Keeping focused on the difference between the kingdom of heaven on earth as Jesus' precious treasure, which he gave us, with all His guarantees of its doctrinal integrity and the Holy Spirit's guidance until the end of time, and the deplorable human elements in that kingdom was not an easy task. It was downright depressing.

15

CONSTANTINE AND POPE SAINT GREGORY THE GREAT

CONSTANTINE AND POPE SAINT GREGORY the Great gave me a lot of headaches. One minute I found myself admiring them, and the next minute I resented the changes they unintentionally caused in Christianity. They both were well intended, and in no way could they begin to imagine the damage that ultimately came from their decisions.

Admirers can write and say what they want about Constantine, but I have developed my own strongly felt conclusions about the man. He was not the first Christian Roman emperor. He was not baptized until almost his deathbed. I still wonder what his real motives were when he made Christianity legal. He did not make it the official religion of the empire, as has been commonly thought. Many things in his life indicate that he was not a practicing Christian. He murdered Licinius, the Eastern Roman emperor, after defeating him, which Constantine promised he would not do. He murdered his wife and son for reasons not known. He was devoted to the pagan god Apollo-Sol, restored the Altar of Victory to the Roman Senate, and authorized payment for the expenses of the pagan religious ceremonies. He did establish Sunday as the official day of worship and allowed wide toleration for Christians and Christian clergy, although he outlawed prose-lytizing by Christians to preserve public order, as many Romans still resented Christianity. Constantine was very involved in Christian theological disputes, more to keep peace among the populace than because he was well versed in or deeply concerned about the substance of the theological matters.

Although he knew little about theology, Constantine called the bishops together at Nicaea in A.D. 325 to settle the hotly debated issue concerning the person and divine attri-butes of Jesus, a dispute brought on by an Alexandrian priest named Arius. The bishops settled the issue at the Council of Nicaea by rejecting Arius' ideas. Nevertheless, before his death Constantine was baptized by the Arian bishop Eusebius of Nicomedia, and he died a peaceful Arian, not believing that Jesus was really of the same nature as God.

But I could understand how a person might say, "So what? Constantine died accepting Jesus. What's all the fuss over a theological theory? It doesn't make any difference to God what theory he believed in."

And many people still think that way, but the issue was im-portant enough for me to try to resolve it for my own peace of mind. Does it make any difference what a person believes as long as the person is close to God and tries to do what is right?

That is something I had to spend a lot of time pondering and, over a long period, trying to resolve. Does it make any difference what we believe, or is God just concerned with how we treat one another?

Going through the gospels over and over to try to see if Jesus confronted this issue in His dealings with the scribes and Pharisees, I found some very interesting parallels. Jesus had a long-drawn-out theological battle with the Jewish people over precisely who He was. He stirred up a tempest when He talked about Himself and His Father being one and then talked about the Holy Spirit being a divine Person. Why did He have to reveal all these things about God that He knew would only cause trouble? And yet He did just that, and eventually it brought about His condemnation for blasphemy. It was, obviously, important to Jesus that people know precisely who He was, and by what authority He was doing and saying the things that He stood for. Everything He said and did witnessed to His identity, and He insisted that people know His origin precisely.

When He offered His flesh and blood as the food that would guarantee eternal life, He insisted that the people accept just what He was saying, and He did not back down when they retorted that it was hard to believe, and who could accept something so ridiculous? He did not give in, and expressed what He meant in stronger language still, even though the whole crowd walked away disillusioned.

And when Peter was struggling with the idea of forgiveness and how many times a person must forgive, he thought he had come a long way when he asked Jesus if seven times was enough. Jesus' response threw Peter into total confusion: "Not seven times, Peter, but seventy times seven times. As often as a person offends you, forgive." Jesus left no room for any other consideration, and Peter just walked away.

When the Samaritan woman at the well asked Jesus where she and her Samaritan friends and neighbors should be worshiping (Samaritans were Israelites who had left the Jewish religion and started their own version of Judaism, though they still used the Jewish Bible), Jesus' answer was unequivocal: "You worship what you do not know. Salvation comes from the Jews"—from Judaism, the religion His Father had established. It is interesting that Jesus would show such respect for the authority of the Jewish religious establishment in Jerusalem even though its leaders treated Him so shamefully. Nevertheless, Jesus still upheld their position as the successors of Moses with the authority from God to teach. They were the magisterium, the official teaching authority in Judaism.

For Jesus it was important that people have definite and clear ideas as to His identity and the precise meaning of His message, and He was loyal to what His Father had established concerning religion. In trying to understand Constantine's acceptance of Arianism, we must ask ourselves: What was the teaching of Arius that the emperor embraced? Arius taught that only the Father was unbegotten and existed from all eternity. At some point the Son was begotten by the Father, so He could not be God, but only the Son of God, since, as Arius held, there was a time when Jesus did not exist. This was the teaching that was forced on the whole empire by imperial decree for all practical purposes. It was mostly through the courage and tenacity of Saint Athanasius, one of the most powerful theologians of the early Church, that Arianism was finally condemned. In the long battle, Athanasius had been exiled five times, once to Trier in Germany, for refusing to accept the Arian view of the nature of Jesus. At one time, later on, he was chased down the Nile River by the Roman army but managed to escape. It is a rather funny story. He realized his small boat could not outrun the military vessel, so after turning around a bend in the river, he and his companions paddled back upriver toward the ship. As they approached, an officer yelled out, asking them if they had seen Bishop Athanasius' boat downriver. "Yes," Athanasius yelled back. "Just a short way down. You should have no trouble catching up with him."

Athanasius fought Constantine and two succeeding emperors and their Arian bishops through five exiles to distant parts of the empire. Only after the rest of the bishops finally mustered up the courage to stand against imperial authority and condemn Arianism by a decision at the Council of Nicaea did Arianism begin to lose ground. It took many more years and the efforts of Athanasius and the Cappadocian Fathers— Saints Basil the Great, Gregory of Nazianzen, and Gregory of Nyssa—to finally defeat Arianism at the Council of Constantinople in A.D. 381. After that it gradually died out. Every now and then, however, the old ideas surface even in modern dress. The teaching of Jehovah's Witnesses, who believe that Jesus was not God originally but was begotten by God, as the firstborn of all creation, and then became God, is similar to Arianism.

What Constantine did accomplish was to give legal standing to the Church so it could grow. The zeal and enthusiasm of the Christians that had been kept pent up for so long while they were persecuted now burst forth in a frenzy of evangelization, which annoyed many of the old Roman aristocracy. Although Constantine forbade Christians from actively seeking converts, it seemed nothing could stop the spread of the Christian message. As that message took hold among even highly placed citizens, and as the numbers mounted, the bishops became more and more powerful not only in Church circles but throughout the empire, both in the East and West. Finally Christianity assumed status as the official imperial religion, replacing worship of the Roman gods. Bishops and priests became imperial officials, and imperial religious laws had to be enacted, with punishments decreed for violations of these laws. Little by little, the beautiful spirit of Jesus faded from sight as the institution became more and more powerful. The Church itself was becoming the message rather than the medium of the message, which is Jesus. Even today when we evangelize we so often end up preaching Church rather than Jesus. The gentle, humble God who came down to earth to teach love and humility seemed and still seems to be an embarrassment to those who enjoy basking in the power and prestige that sets them above people.

Constantine's favoring Christianity necessarily led to the Church's supremacy throughout the empire. That was devastating to Jesus' understanding of what Church should be: a family of caring people, worshiping God together as a family, not an imperial institution ruling over people's lives. Jesus certainly never intended that bishops become imperial religious officials issuing decrees and lording it over their flock. Constantine certainly did not do God a favor. We are still paying the price for that "favor."

What Constantine did by decree, Pope Saint Gregory the Great followed up by his genius as an administrator. He was one of the holiest and most brilliant of the popes, and led the Church wisely and with great humility through extremely difficult times. On the death of Gregory's father, a Roman senator, his mother retired to religious life to do charitable works. Gregory distributed his wealth to help the poor and converted his estate into a monastery, which he entered as a simple monk.

Later he was ordained a deacon and sent as ambassador of the pope to Constantinople. Recalled from there six years later, he was elected pope shortly afterward, and set an example of holiness and humble concern for the people under his care. His many writings were to influence the Church for centuries. One of his most important works is on the care of souls and the responsibilities of bishops and clergy for the needs of the people.

Even though he was such a great saint, his being forced by circumstances to care for the temporal needs of the people of Rome and its surrounding areas introduced the Church to temporal power and set it on a course that was to have a devastating effect on it. Gregory was elected pope at a critical time, not just for the Church but for Rome as well. Constantine had abandoned Rome in favor of Byzantium, which he built up into a magnificent city and renamed Constantinople. Rome was without an army, without a police force, and the city and its inhabitants fell prey to hordes of barbarians and brigands. Gregory, who had been an official in the imperial government and was one of the few important people left in Rome with administrative talent and experience, was pressured by the citizens to do something to protect them. His family was wealthy and possessed extensive agricultural lands in Africa. Elected pope by acclamation, Gregory could not avoid doing something to protect the people, so he organized a small army to secure the city. In gratitude, people left land and property to him as pope. That wealth was the origin of much abuse on the part of papal authorities. The Vatican accumulated more and more property, which ultimately over the centuries evolved into the Papal States, something that would have saddened Jesus. From that time on, the Church became even more powerful; eventually the pope had control of much of the politics of Europe, not exactly what Jesus intended for his Church. We are still struggling to free ourselves from that sad departure from the gentle, humble Jesus, who taught by humility and the beauty of his own life, not by the trappings of power and majesty. I hope that one day a generation of humble shepherds will appear among the flock and guide it with the meekness of the Good Shepherd and again change the course of the Church's history.

I have to admit I am embarrassed that at one time I took pride in the fact that the Church had so much power. As I grew older I realized that that power was just the thing that Jesus did *not* want for His Church. He tried so hard to teach the apostles a humble understanding of authority, as if He knew that in only a few generations preoccupation with temporal cares and concerns would become overwhelming and that leaders would only too easily assume the power that was theirs for the taking. With that, Jesus' beautiful dream of humble shepherds began to fade and all but disappear.

16

THE MYSTERY OF
THE CHURCH

*t*HE EARLY CHURCH FATHERS performed a remarkable task in defining the identity not only of Jesus for future generations of His followers, but also of the Church, setting before us Jesus' vision of the Church and its place in the life of the Christian people. Their struggle in accomplishing these critical feats was a reflection of the struggles of many of the earliest Christians to understand their own beliefs and what it was precisely that they were expected to believe as Christians. Who is Jesus, and what is Church? It is a struggle that all Christians have to face in trying to find a reason for our own faith, and what precisely is the meaning of Jesus as Savior and Son of God and what Jesus as Son of God expects of us.

Jesus defined the Church in parables. Whenever He told a parable about the kingdom of heaven, He was talking about the kingdom of heaven on earth, the Church He was founding. Jesus had no illusions about the Church; He could be brutally realistic in describing what this Church was going to be like. On one occasion He said the Church is like a merchant in search of fine pearls. One day he found this stunning pearl and sold all he had to purchase it. On another occasion Jesus compared the Church to a man who came upon a treasure hidden in a field. He sold all he had and purchased that field. This kingdom of heaven, this Church, is so important in our lives that it is worth sacrificing everything else in order to possess it. After saying these wonderful things about the Church, Jesus then told people parables of a different aspect of the Church. It is like a farmer who sowed wheat in his field. One night the enemy came and sowed weeds. To his surprise, the farmer later found that the wheat was full of weeds. He told his farm hands to let it go until harvest time; then he would separate the wheat from the weeds. Another parable said the Church is like a fisherman who came back with a large catch of fish. He sorted the fish as he sat onshore. He put the good fish in baskets to be brought to market. But some of the fish stank to high heaven; those he threw away.

These parables were strong warnings to all of us not to expect too much from the Church. It is divine in one way. It is the living presence of Jesus throughout history, but it is also human, and that human element in the Church can be the cause of much pain and discouragement. Nevertheless, the Church is still the precious pearl of great price, still worth our possessing it, and there is never a logical reason to reject it. It is the body of Christ and the bride of Christ, and has within it all Jesus' treasures for us. Like any family, in many ways it is dysfunctional, but it is our family. To walk away and think we can do better than what Jesus gave us is not possible. The new community will eventually wither, like a branch cut off the vine, as Jesus warned.

The Fathers of the Church were very well aware of both these aspects that Jesus talked about. They took Jesus' visions of Church for granted. Their concern was how the Church should function on a day-to-day basis, or how Jesus structured the Church to assure its survival until the end of time. Since many of the early Fathers knew apostles or their immediate disciples, they were very well aware of the apostles' understanding of how the Church should be structured and operate.

At first, the Fathers' vision of the Church may seem rigid, with little room for any other model. They saw the Church as governed by apostles and those they chose as successors, and over whom they prayed and laid hands, calling down the power of the Holy Spirit. The apostles and their successors—bishops, as they called them—stood in the place of Jesus. For a Christian worship assembly to be valid, the people had to be one with their bishop. Apart from their bishop, the Eucharist could not be pleasing to God. Individuals spreading doctrines differing from the traditional teachings handed down from Jesus through the apostles and the bishops were, in the eyes of the Fathers, wolves in sheep's clothing tearing apart the flock. The bishop was the bond that united the community with God and made their worship pleasing and acceptable to God. What would the Fathers think of the proliferation of Christian churches today, teaching over two thousand versions of Jesus' message, especially as conscious as the Fathers were of Jesus' desperate prayer for unity just before He died? This fragmentation of the message helped me appreciate the value of the Fathers' clear-cut image of Church. In its simplicity, it was pure and unpolitical. It was pure because the Fathers' understanding came directly from the mouths of the apostles and was an uncomplicated reflection of how Jesus saw His Church. They had no vested interest, had no need to develop a new theology to justify novel personal beliefs. They could honestly stick with the simple vision of Church passed on from the beginning. Only later did the image become blurred when a different definition was needed to satisfy political, ethnic, or personal demands of people disillusioned by scandal. Then the definition of Church was determined by what people wanted Church to be, rather than by what had been passed down from Jesus through the apostles and the Church Fathers.

Trying to understand the Church was not an easy exercise for me. In my later seminary days, I realized that one of the most important decisions I had to make as a Christian was whether I was going to follow what pleased me about church and religion, or whether I would take the time and trouble to find out what God expected of me. The latter choice was not easy. It places a lifelong burden on a person.

In the Old Testament, God establishes the religion. Today people start their own religions and tell God how they want to worship Him. In the Bible, it is God who tells His creatures how He wants us to relate to Him. He is the Creator; we are the creatures with the responsibility to respond to God's wishes. The temptation is always to tell God how we will worship Him and what the form of our worship will be, and what pleases us. That's not the way it is. The responsibility lies in our hearts to worship God the way He shows us.

This is not an easy task. In worshiping God, we belong to

community, the community of God's family. We are brothers and sisters in the family of faith, a family in which no one is a stranger. We are members of the mystical body of Jesus, which bonds us together with responsibilities to care for one another. To guide, nourish, and direct the family, God placed clergy as shepherds of the flock. Some are kind and good and caring; many are obnoxious. Clergy in our parishes are no different from us. Some are holy to a great degree; some seem little interested in spiritual matters or even in those under their care. Some have pleasant, caring personalities; some have personalities like guard dogs.

When it comes to bishops, the situation is the same. They are human with all the traits that other humans have. They can be warm, courteous, and approachable, or they can be cold, distant, and aloof. Some care deeply for the people; others may be interested only in personal advancement in their chosen field of politics, which, unfortunately for hurting sheep, is the Church. For them, compassion is dangerous; it can trick them into making a politically incorrect mistake, by bending a law to help someone, and jeopardize their chance for advancement. Sadly, they are often the ones who advance rapidly because they can be counted on never to make a mistake. They have done more damage to the Church than any questionable theologian. It is not easy to develop healthy attitudes toward all these leaders who deeply affect our religious and spiritual lives. Many people cannot make the adjustments necessary and leave the Church. Others bear with the difficulties and detach themselves from the life of the Church while still attending Mass and receiving the sacraments. Some lose heart and just go through the motions of being observant, worshiping on Christmas, Easter, and maybe Ash Wednesday and Palm Sunday.

It is not easy to live within the Church. The Church is a most difficult society precisely because of its mission. Its mission is to gather together the sheep in a flock with all types of sheep, the good and the bad, the sleek and the crippled, the hurting and the healthy. If the Church is doing its job, it will always be full of sinners, from top to bottom. And a family full of sinners will, even at its best, be a dysfunctional one. A dysfunctional family does not make for easy living; every member has to learn to adjust to difficult personalities.

It took me many painful years to understand the Church and my own place in it. Life in the monastery was beautiful, but not easy. Making the adjustments to living with strangers having widely diverse personalities was possible only with the help of massive doses of divine grace. As a priest I had to find my place in the Church and determine a set of attitudes that would make living in it reasonable and healthy for me.

It was difficult for me to understand the hard, inflexible attitudes of some Vatican officials. I had seen those rigid types of personalities in the seminary and in the monastery. Their inflexibility, not theological but psychological, was based on fear and need for security—hanging on to things taught to us since childhood by parents or by parish priests who may not even have been well versed in theology. But it was not the Church's theology that troubled me. What troubled me was how I handled statements of psychologically rigid theologians when I knew that the theology they expressed was not defined teachings of the Church. Knowing that these theologians taught very different opinions before they became Vatican officials troubled me even more and struck me as insincere and dishonest. I could not respect the opinions they were now expressing because I knew that, deep down, they did not believe them themselves. Having kept abreast of theology and being current on present-day developments, I knew what was authentic and what was only theological opinion. What troubled me most deeply were officials trying to force theologians to accept and adhere to the opinions of radically conservative colleagues. The tactics they used bordered on bullying. Even back in the earliest days of the Church, the popes allowed the bishops and theologians to debate the issues, sometimes over the course of many years, and in this way clarify those issues to the point where a wise and prudent conclusion could be settled on and accepted by the vast majority of bishops. That is the proper way to develop understanding and consensus, not force opinions on the whole Church when they are not yet even defined.

What is improper in the procedure today is that the bishops and, to a greater and greater degree, theologians are kept out of the debate, and issues are unilaterally decided and promulgated by the Congregation of the Doctrines of the Faith, supposedly with the Holy Father's knowing approval, and imposed on the bishops.

I wonder sometimes, especially lately, if the Holy Father even has the energy to read all the material placed before him, or whether he just trusts his officials' honesty when they place things before him to sign. For officials to improperly assume authority violates the authority Jesus gave to the bishops as successors of the apostles. Jesus appointed the apostles and Peter as their head to guide and teach the flock until the end of time. The apostles are still here, and Peter in the person of the pope is still here. It is the bishops together with the pope who have the right and the authority under the guidance of the Holy Spirit, as Jesus promised, to formulate and disseminate teachings and to rule the Church. To cut the bishops off from this process is an abuse of authority.

Unfortunately, the bishops seem to do nothing about it. I hope it is not fear that they might jeopardize their promotions or be censured for insubordination that prevents them from speaking out. Sadly, bishops seem to have lost a sense of their own authority as successors of the apostles, which should give them the backbone to speak their minds without fear, out of loyalty to Jesus, as did Saint Cyprian. Cyprian wrote telling the pope that he respected him as the Bishop of Rome and the successor of Peter as head of the Church, but that he also insisted that the pope respect him as a successor of the apostles and not interfere in the running of his diocese in North Africa. That is the proper understanding of the relationship between pope and bishops.

The Vatican Curia (the pope's cabinet) serves in a secretarial role as advisors and counselors to the pope. They have no official teaching authority of their own. Curial officials still should defer to the bishops, whose authority comes from Jesus. If the various congregations provided guidelines to the bishops, that would be proper. Currently the Curia issues mandates and directives to the bishops; these actions demean the authority Jesus gave to the apostles. Even Saint Peter, who was well aware of his authority, was more respectful of the independence and authority of the other apostles. As the apostles were in their own time, so their successors, the bishops today, are the teachers and the guides of the faithful, not the Curia. The bishops know what decisions have to be made for the health of their dioceses. Only if a bishop is seriously delinquent in fulfilling his responsibilities should others interfere.

Some might say, "What they do in Rome doesn't affect you, so it's really none of your business. Why let it bother you?" Everything that happens in the Church is the business of every one of us, especially if we are aware of the way things should be. What affects the health of part of the Church affects all of us, and we need to make our feelings known. It is difficult to feel at peace when something is wrong at such critical levels of the Church.

While the Vatican's treatment of bishops did not affect me, it severely restricted bishops' freedom to make decisions and set policy necessary for their own dioceses, where centuries-old customs and traditions vary from place to place around the world. Life in the United States has situations unparalleled in most other parts of the world. World War II had a dramatic effect on Christians of all denominations in this country. Servicemen and -women of various denominations and religions fought side by side. They took care of each other when they were wounded or dying. Deep affection and comradeship soon replaced the old religious prejudices, and they came back home after the war and became godparents for each other's children. The old walls of suspicion and prejudice had changed.

During the war, the troops shared each other's chaplains. They cared for each other when they were wounded. They comforted one another when they were dying in the killing fields. They saw goodness in each other and elements in each other's religions that were good and healthy. A new spirit of ecumenism took hold spontaneously. It was not a watering down of faith or a loosening of attachment to one's religion. It was a beautiful sharing of what was good in the different ways we all worshiped God and lived our faith.

Unfortunately, elements in the European hierarchy in the Vatican took exception to this new interdenominational intimacy and looked on American Catholics as soft on doctrine and too willing to accommodate Protestant practices, including Protestant hymns in Catholic services, and to participate in each other's religious services. Their insistence on publicizing restrictions on Communion to Protestants has caused much misunderstanding and strained what had been a warm bond leading to closer unity. It served only to show that some are not yet ready for real steps toward unity, but only talk. I cannot help but wonder if we wouldn't rather talk about unity than do something positive to bring it about. I wonder why some Vatican officials are so rigid about not giving Communion to Protestant Christians who believe in Jesus' real presence in the Eucharist when the Holy Father himself gave Communion to Lutheran bishops when they came to Mass in his private chapel. I learned that the pope had done this from friends who participated in the service.

This issue has bothered me for years because it is not an honest policy. There does not seem to be a theological reason why a Christian who believes in the real presence of Jesus in the Eucharist cannot receive the Eucharist in our Church. The argument is given that they don't accept *all* our teachings. If that is the litmus test, then perhaps, out of a sense of honesty, we should test our own parishioners and see how many don't accept all the teachings of the Church. I wonder how many more Catholics we could exclude from Communion.

While lack of respect for the authority of bishops on the part of the Vatican is a serious problem, it certainly was not a matter that affected my faith. In my writings, however, I try to emphasize the seriousness of the problem in the hope that someday it will be corrected.

What is more upsetting is the relationship between bishops and their priests, and pastors and their parishioners. In a diocese, especially in a small one, it would seem that the bishop would have a personal relationship with each of his priests. Not that they would be close personal friends, but the bishop would, perhaps, make an effort to get to know his priests personally rather than depend on passing comments, either good or bad, in making judgments about them. In my travels around the country and abroad, I learned a lot from priests who told me about their problems and frustrations. They felt their bishop did not have the slightest idea of the work they were doing in their parish and did not even care. They told me how much they wished their bishop could see what was happening and how much they craved some kind of approval from him—or even a simple acknowledgment that he was aware of their efforts. In most cases it never came. So many priests felt that the bishop did not have the slightest interest in what individual priests were doing, as long as they kept out of trouble. Administration of the diocesan machinery was each bishop's overriding concern.

Learning all of these things made me realize how lonely most priests were. Many felt that the only concern of the diocese was that the priests meet their assessments on time and respond promptly to any requests from diocesan offices. Of course, those priests who had known the bishop since seminary days had a more personal relationship with him. Their situations were more rewarding, and their life in a particular diocese was more enjoyable. They could not understand why others should have negative feelings.

Life was similar in monasteries. Monastic life is a beautiful way of living—it provides the setting for quiet and solitude, and concentrated spiritual growth. The Eucharistic Presence of Jesus in the chapel offers many occasions during the day, or night, to drop in for a visit to pray or just be there with Jesus. The thrice-daily community chanting of the divine office, the official prayer of the Church, is a powerful source of strength. Even when I was depressed, the daily morning and evening meditation focused the day around God and, in spite of my discouragement, made me aware that He was never far away, even at times when I doubted His closeness. A peaceful and secure feeling came from that kind of regularly scheduled prayer, and it helped to compensate for my own personal anguish.

You might think that living with thirty or forty strangers day after day would be psychologically impossible. Surprisingly, in time we adjusted to daily living with so many entirely different personalities, some likable, some miserable. We gradually learned to look on and accept all as brothers, and even benefit from the diversity. We all learned a lot from each other.

Relationships with superiors were a different matter. Some were kind and understanding. We could talk to them and feel they were sincerely interested in the spiritual growth of those of us under their charge. Others had difficult personalities. Why we elected them to their positions is beyond me, as some did not seem very interested in the religious life and even less interested in the members of the community whose spiritual life was supposed to be their prime concern. I had always believed a religious superior would be a person who took the time to know each monk. I imagined the superior would casually meet with each one on a regular basis to be a support and guide in his spiritual life, to help him find an assignment best suited to his personality and in which he could make the best contribution to the community and grow personally in the process.

Yet it never turned out that way. I blame myself for having had unrealistic expectations. Nevertheless, life in the monastery was still beautiful. Even though I have now been away from it for forty years, I still have feelings of nostalgia when I think of my years as a monk. I cherish the pleasant memories of the comradeship and fun with all the diverse personalities, which prevented the life from ever being boring. How many times I have been tempted to go back to it!

17

CHRISTIAN MARRIAGE AND THE EUCHARIST

*A*S I HAVE MENTIONED, I made my First Holy Communion when I was seven years old. It had such an effect on my life as a child that I used to get up every morning and go to Mass so I could receive Jesus in Communion. That need for intimacy with Jesus has lasted all through my life. When I became a pastor for the first time, I wanted so much to be able to instill in the little children a deep love of Jesus in the Eucharist. From my experience in various parishes, I was saddened to notice that within a few weeks after the children made their First Communion, they stopped going not just to Communion but to church. I could never understand why the children did not have the same need to receive Communion that I had as a child. Something had to be wrong. Perhaps it was in the way we prepare the children for their reception of the Eucharist.

At the same time, I also realized that perhaps 40 percent of the people in the parish were divorced and remarried without the Church's blessing. Most of them were not going to church either. That explained a lot. How could I expect the children to come to Mass and receive Communion if their parents did not come and receive? I tried everything to encourage the young people to understand what Communion was. I used to gather the little children up around the altar for part of the Mass so they could feel close to what was happening. They loved that. Many of the kids would wake their parents up on Sunday mornings so they could go to church and stand around the altar with me, which did not make me very popular with some of the fathers.

One little boy used to ask his parents if he could go swimming in the pool in the backyard. When they said yes, he put on his trunks and went out to the yard, then slipped out through the gate and ran to the church, where he would come in the back door and see if I was at the altar. As soon as he spotted me, he would run up the aisle, hug me, and ask if he could serve my Mass. When I smiled yes, he would go into the sacristy, put on a little altar boy's robe, and come back out to help me. He loved to receive Communion. And I am sure Jesus loved being with little Jimmy as well.

One other little child, Stacy, used to come to church all by herself after she received her First Communion. Her parents did not come very often, so she walked up to church by herself and at Communion time came up to the altar to receive Jesus. Those two little children were such a comfort to me. They are both thirty years older now. Stacy lives in Las Vegas. I hope she gets in touch with me some day. Jimmy still lives with his mother. Others also were very faithful, but those two were special, and since it was a small parish, everyone at Mass knew them and was deeply moved by seeing them come to church each Sunday. I saw Jimmy not too long ago when he and his mother came to a talk I gave. That was the first time in almost twenty-five years that we had seen each other. I recognized him right away, and we both hugged just like when he was a little boy. And we still both felt the same about each other. His mother told me that he never forgot me and wanted so much to come to the talk.

How to get the children in my parishes to receive Communion was always on my mind. Knowing that their parents' marriage situation was part of the problem, I tried to encourage them to apply for annulments. Some were open to it. Many were too shy or introverted to discuss their personal married lives with clergy. Some were married to Protestants, and often the Protestant party was reluctant. They could not understand why such a procedure was necessary. Also, the procedure was too complicated and took too long. I interviewed many of the parents privately and realized they had very good reason to end their first marriage and that their second marriage was for them a blessing. Someday, I hope, the Vatican and the bishops will simplify the annulment procedure. With all the annulments currently needed in our parishes, it would take fifty years to process them all. Who can wait fifty years to get their marriage blessed?

I also changed the way we did First Communion. I started a six-week program to train the parents to teach their own children about Communion. This was a mini-course on the basic beliefs of a Catholic Christian. The last week concentrated on how the parents could make Communion a warm, intimate friendship with Jesus. Then the parents had to prepare their own children for Communion. When they thought the children were ready, they would call and bring them in to be interviewed. After assuring myself that the children realized what Holy Communion was, I would ask if they had done anything in their lives that would have hurt Jesus, and I would help them examine their consciences. I was surprised at the things they told me, which convinced me that they understood they were telling God they were sorry for things they had done wrong. Then I gave them absolution. The following Sunday the whole family would receive Communion together. Sometimes it took some strong encouragement, especially with some of the fathers, but afterward they all told me that it was a wonderful experience for them and that they felt so good that they had received Communion with their son or daughter.

After all the children had made their First Communion, we had a class Communion Sunday and a breakfast in the parish hall. Sunday after Sunday, many of those little children would wake up their parents and embarrass them into taking them to Mass.

The problem of parents' annulments still bothers me because it is a major problem that the Church is not facing realistically. There are millions of people needing annulments, which is a serious impediment to the healthy life of every parish and undermines the whole life of the Church. The people do not feel good about themselves, yet it is not practical to encourage them all to apply for annulments, not only because the process takes so long but because so many possible applicants have difficult situations with a past spouse. One couple who applied were told to contact their previous spouses. The man's former wife was dead. The woman's previous spouse was long gone, and she could not contact him. He would not have been cooperative anyway. The couple were then told it would not be possible for them to receive an annulment. Shortly thereafter they left the Catholic Church and joined the Methodist Church, which really upset me because I had worked with them for two years. The man was very sick and did not have long to live; he wanted to do the right thing and apply for the annulment. I recommended against it because I felt it would be a dangerously stressful experience. It was. He died not long after the episode.

People's lives are often so complicated. So many people have been hurt and damaged since childhood that there has to be a much more flexible process to reconcile them so they can receive the sacraments. They are precisely the ones who need the love and warmth of Jesus in the Eucharist. If we look at their situations through the eyes of the Good Shepherd, it is not right to say they cannot receive Communion. The Good Shepherd went out and looked for the lost, the troubled, the bruised and hurting sheep the Pharisees alienated, and placed them on His shoulders and carried them back home, because, as He said, "He loved the sheep." These people know if their first marriage was a healthy, viable relationship or unhealthy and destructive from the start. Who can say they are living in sin if in good conscience they make a decision that they think to be an honest one?

I am not saying that we should abolish the annulment process, because I know it has been a great help to many people considering a future relationship. The annulment process can help people to avoid whatever may have caused problems in their previous marriage.

Another question tied up with marriage situations is the requirement for the ceremony. We tell people that they have to be married before a priest or a deacon; otherwise their marriage is invalid and will not be recognized by the Church. Why does that have to be required? If they don't marry before a priest, why do we have to say they are living in sin? Many people are not ready or not mature enough in their faith to appreciate a religious ceremony. Why do we have to demand it? A Christian marriage service is a beautiful way to begin a married life, but not everyone today is spiritually mature enough to appreciate it. If a man and a woman choose to make a commitment to each other in the presence of God, before a priest and the community of friends, that is beautiful and could inspire others to choose to be married in a religious ceremony. But to demand it does not seem right. If it is chosen freely because a couple believe it is an ideal way to begin their life together, that is a wonderful witness to the whole community. Demanding a ceremony before a priest for people who, in their hearts, may not want that kind of ceremony and have not the slightest interest in things spiritual does not always have the desired effect. I have witnessed conversations and events just before wedding ceremonies that made me humiliated and ashamed that I had to be a part of such an empty formality. Requiring that couples be married before a priest or deacon, when so many couples are not ready for that, is pushing them to reject the Church and be cut off from the sacraments. This is having a devastating effect on millions of children and jeopardizes the future health of the Church. It wasn't always required that people marry before a priest. To invalidate a couple's relationship because they do not marry before a priest and to deny them Communion for that reason does not seem to make good spiritual sense. I am not saying this practice is right. I am not saying it is wrong. I am just suggesting that the whole issue be thoroughly reviewed so we can be much more honest and realistic in our approach to something so sacred as a lifelong commitment in a bond of mutual love.

Requiring an annulment before people remarry often pushes people into very difficult situations, as the process takes so long. The annulment procedure has to be simplified to facilitate the rectifying of these critical situations in people's lives. The slow and inefficient procedure is doing untold damage to the Church and creating a situation where almost half the Catholic people are second-class members in the Church. Many feel that belonging to another church is more attractive because they can at least receive the Eucharist and create a more spiritually wholesome family life for their children.

I pose this thought: Suppose the Church did not require that people marry before a priest or deacon, and a marriage before a judge was allowed without requiring previous Church approval. Suppose further that a couple's marriage broke up and ended in divorce, even though the couple were good people who made every effort to make the marriage work. Finally they realized that there was something intrinsically wrong with the marriage from the start, and it was not a healthy, workable relationship and was doing serious damage to each of them. If they should then decide to marry other persons in the presence of a judge or a minister, would the Church look on the marriage as invalid and their relationships sinful? If the Church would look on it as sinful, why would it be considered so? Because the couple did not get an annulment? If the Church does not make a marriage null, but merely makes a decision that it was null from the beginning, should not the couple themselves know that the marriage was null? And if, knowing that, they decide to marry again, why should they be considered to be living in sin? Just because they decided not to apply for an annulment? Should they then be denied Communion just because they did not apply for an annulment?

I pose these questions and pursue the issue because something has to be done to clear up this frightfully damaging situation we are now facing in the Church. Church officials themselves are sinfully delinquent if they can so easily tolerate a situation where almost half the Church is cut off from receiving the Eucharist, which Jesus said is essential for eternal life. Would the Good Shepherd say, "I am the Good Shepherd. I go out and search for the lost, the troubled, the bruised and hurting sheep. When I find them I pick them up, place them on my shoulders and carry them back home." After bringing them back home, would he say, "All right, now you go and sit in the corner there, while the rest of us have our supper"? Is that what He would say? If the Good Shepherd chooses to embrace sinners, how can we say they are not worthy of His embrace?

In choosing to meet the Samaritan woman at the well, Jesus did so for a reason. He had already preached a high ideal of marriage, but still decided to meet this woman, who had

been married five times, as He said, and "the one you are living with now is not your husband." He did not approve of her
many marriages, but He still admitted they were marriages
and still chose her to announce the good news to that town.
And the gospel does not say He told her to leave the man she
was living with. Jesus knew only too well what the conse-
quences would be for the woman if he demanded that. The
difference between Jesus and so many Church leaders is that
Jesus could preach high ideals, then turn around and show exquisite compassion to people who fell far short of those ideals.
Church leaders preach high ideals but fall far short in showing compassion to people who do not measure up to those
ideals. Like the scribes and Pharisees, Church leaders feel a
need to punish them. I am not saying that Church leaders are
hypocrites, but that we treat people as the Pharisees did. Why
can we not be more like the Good Shepherd in our understanding and compassion for people with problems? Why do
we feel a need to censure rather than to heal? Why do we feel
it necessary to deny Jesus to people who are at a time in their
lives when they need Him the most? If the Good Shepherd
chose to go and search for sinners and then embrace them,
should we not allow Him still to embrace them, rather than
say they are unworthy of His embrace? Jesus described
Himself as the Good Shepherd to show that He was different
from the scribes and Pharisees who cut people off from temple worship because they were unworthy. There are so many
damaged and crippled souls today. They need more understanding and healing, not punishment and further rejection.

This issue has assaulted my loyalty to Church leaders and
caused me much pain and anguish as a pastor. Why do legal-

ists have to treat people this way? Why this terrible need to punish? Some may say, "They can get an annulment if they want." That is no solution if you are really concerned about bringing the millions of hurting people back to the sacraments. Of course, if you don't care, then any solution, no matter how inadequate, is acceptable.

From my experience with Protestant parishes and difficult personal situations in many of those parishes, I was impressed with the courtesy and Christ-like manner in which their ministers treat their people. Although often the ministers' wives call them to task when they are not courteous or are brusque, most often compassion is the ordinary procedure in those churches. The clergy seem to be much more caring of their people and try to make an effort to reach out to them when they are hurting. Even denominations that do not accept or approve of divorce have a much more compassionate way of treating their people than we do in our Church.

Did noticing the difference shake my faith? No, but it shook my confidence, and still shakes my confidence, in our Church officials, who treat almost half the Church's membership so insensitively and by so doing seriously damage the spiritual health of the whole mystical Body of Jesus and threaten the future of the Church itself. If Jesus could encourage the people to respect the scribes and Pharisees because they succeeded to Moses' authority in spite of the shabby way they treated Him and the people as well, then out of loyalty to Jesus I can follow His example and offer my little contribution to make the Church He gave us a better reflection of His image as Good Shepherd.

18

THE CHURCH
AND SCRIPTURE

ONE OF THE OLDEST MEMORIES I have of my father
goes back to my childhood. I remember him on Sunday after-
noons lying on the sofa, reading the Bible, especially the
gospels. He was reading about Jesus. That made a lasting impression on me. The only other material I ever remember him
reading was the life of Thomas Jefferson and the American
Constitution. From those sources he got the courage and the
wisdom to challenge the law that forbade school districts from
giving textbooks to Catholic schools and other church-run
schools. Not only did he and my little brother go to the
Supreme Court and challenge the law, but they won the case.
When I got older and entered the seminary, my father gave
me two books, which I treasured: *The Imitation of Christ,* by
Thomas à Kempis, and *Words of Encouragement,* by Father
Daniel Considine.

My father was a very down-to-earth man, a manly person, practical and very efficient. He had a deep love of the Catholic Church and a great respect for priests and bishops, even though he was aware of their human failings. Whenever we would get upset with the Church, he would always say, "It's not the Church that's bad, it's people. Jesus gave us the Church. It's His gift to us. It's people who do bad things."

My father never said much, but what he did say was very much to the point and you could never forget it. He taught us that the Church was sacred and that, as Jesus said, "The kingdom of heaven, the Church, is the pearl of great price, for which a man went out and sold all he had to possess it."

Later on, as a teenager, I heard a Protestant minister on the radio saying that the Church was evil, that it was not faithful to Christ, and that Catholics could not go to heaven because they did not follow the Bible. That confused me; I could not understand why he would say a thing like that. We do read the Bible in church every Sunday morning, and the priest read the Bible at Mass every morning when I went to church, and my father read the Bible faithfully, and my parents always talked to us, the twelve of us, about Jesus.

When I went into the seminary, we read the Bible and had talks and retreats based on stories in the Bible. We had intensive scripture courses and studied the Bible thoroughly. Our professors were well-known scripture scholars. I told this to a fundamentalist I was talking to one day, and he said that even if we do read the Bible, we do not base our faith on the Bible. It is necessary to base your faith on the Bible and all that the Bible teaches. The Bible is the sole rule of faith, not the Church. That is what his church teaches its members.

That remark finally made me understand all the other comments and criticisms I had heard. Now, at least, I had something to hang on to and to study. What is the basis of our faith? Is it the Bible, or is it the Church? I had to know once and for all, and settle this issue.

It is true Saint Paul says, "All scripture is inspired." But when Saint Paul said that, he was referring to the Old Testament, because there was no New Testament yet. The gospels and other books of the New Testament had not yet been put together. What letters and gospels and other writings that existed were not yet looked on as scripture, on the same level as the Old Testament. Then I went through the New Testament to find where Jesus told anyone to write any inspired books or to add to the Bible or to write a New Testament. I could find no justification for people saying that the Bible is the sole rule of faith. I asked people where that came from and could not get a definite answer. They kept saying that Saint Paul says that "all scripture is inspired."

"But," I replied, "there was no New Testament in existence when Saint Paul spoke those words."

At that point there was silence.

"But everybody knows that the whole Bible is inspired," some responded.

"But it is important to know who decided it was inspired," I said. "Someone with authority had to declare it was inspired; otherwise how can we use it as the sole rule of faith? Did Jesus ever tell anyone to write a New Testament with all the books and tell people that is all they need as a guide?"

"Our minister told us that the Bible is the inspired word of God."

That still did not answer my question. I was determined to find the answer to the question: What is the place of the Bible in the life of Christians? This is a critical issue for all Christians. Why should I put faith solely in a book if I am not solidly convinced that it is something different from every other good spiritual book I have read and that God *demanded* that I use that book alone as the guide for my life?

Struggling with this question was important. I had encountered so many people who were told that the Catholic Church went wrong because it was teaching doctrines that were not in the Bible and things that Jesus never talked about in the gospels. The question in my mind, however, was deeper than that. Can I *assume* that the Bible was written as the only guide in matters of faith? In the Old Testament there was the Bible, and that was not the sole guide. Jesus told His disciples to do what the scribes and Pharisees taught because they occupied the chair of Moses. They had been authorized by God to teach. John also mentions about Caiaphas prophesying that one man must die for the nation so the whole nation does not perish. John said he prophesied because he was the high priest of that time. Also, much of what was in the Bible had been oral tradition for hundreds of years prior to its being written down. The high priests, scribes, and Pharisees were the ones authorized by God to interpret what was written down; in fact, previous scribes and priests were the ones who actually put the oral traditions in written form.

Neither in the writings of the apostles nor in the gospels could I find any place where Jesus told someone to add something to the already existing Bible, so the problem of authority was for me still unresolved. My attachment to the Church, instilled in me from childhood, was the only authority I knew. Was I right in believing that the Church had the responsibility and the authority to teach?

Nowhere could I find evidence that God told anyone that the New Testament was the only valid witness to Jesus and what He taught and that the Bible was the only authority needed to guide our lives. I could not find a justification for that belief anywhere. I could see the Bible as a most important means of learning about God and Jesus and the things that Jesus said and did, but I could find no justification for it being the only rule of faith. Only in reading the life of Martin Luther did I finally find a statement expressing that idea, and that was written fifteen hundred years after Christianity had come into existence. It was certainly not a part of what Jesus taught, nor did Saint Paul or the other apostles teach it, nor was it a part of what any of the disciples of the apostles, the early Fathers of the Church, taught.

So, my questions still remained: What are we supposed to believe? Did Jesus authorize a teaching guide, or did He leave the survival of His teachings up to chance that people would just learn them on their own?

To solve these questions to my personal satisfaction, I knew I could not use the New Testament alone, because there was no New Testament when Jesus was alive. Thus He could not have said the New Testament should be the sole rule of faith. If the apostles had told their disciples that the gospels and other writings by the apostles should be the sole rule of faith, then that would be good evidence. I really needed sources outside of scripture, sources close to those who knew Jesus and knew what He had taught.

I wanted to determine if they taught anything about authority, and where authority exists in the Christian community, that I could use to verify what might have been said in the gospels or in other books of the New Testament.

Again I resorted to the earliest Fathers of the Church. Saint Polycarp was a disciple of Saint John. Who among the apostles knew the mind of Jesus better than Saint John? Saint Ignatius of Antioch was another source that would be important in resolving this issue.

In my studies of these men and other Church Fathers, I could find nothing about scripture being the sole rule of faith, the authority on which all our Christian beliefs must be based. There was no New Testament yet, only some letters and a few manuscripts that were beginning to circulate. It was clear, however, that the Fathers consistently backed the authority of the apostles and the bishops who succeeded them as having authority from Jesus to teach and to guide the Church. Nowhere do the apostles or any of the Fathers of the Church say that sacred scripture is the sole rule of faith. In fact, nowhere does even Saint Paul say that the Bible is the rule of faith. Saint Paul does say, however, that faith comes through hearing, and all the earliest Christian converts were converted through hearing the message of Jesus spoken to them by the apostles. As there was no New Testament for many years, the early Christians did not use the New Testament as their sole rule of faith. Their faith came to them through the apostles, the bishops, and the priests who taught them. They learned through listening and hearing.

Even as late as the year A.D. 200 there was no complete New Testament scripture. Not until late in the fourth century did the Church recognize as inspired sacred writings the twenty-seven books that we now have in the New Testament. And Saint Augustine remarked that he accepted the New Testament as the inspired word of God "because the Church told me so."

Augustine realized that only someone with authority from God to teach could declare that the New Testament is the inspired word of God; otherwise no one would have the obligation to accept it. So the bottom line is that the scriptures are endorsed by the authority given to the Church by Jesus, which makes them important in our lives as Christians. But it is clear that the most fundamental authority in Christianity resides not in the Bible—which Jesus never told anyone to write—but in the apostles, headed by Peter, and their successors down through the centuries.

As Jesus said to the apostles, "Go out and teach all nations whatsoever I have taught you. Those who accept you, accept me, those who refuse to accept you, refuse to accept me." Most of the books of the New Testament can be accepted as solid teaching because they were written by the apostles. Luke and Mark were not apostles; they are accepted as sacred writers because of the authority of the Church. If the Church had no authority to teach that the New Testament is inspired, then no one has any obligation to accept it as inspired. And if anyone asks why you accept the Bible and the New Testament as the inspired word of God, the only valid answer is because the Church, which has authority from Jesus, says they are inspired. No one else could ever make that statement because no one else had authority to do so. It does not make sense to accept the Bible as the inspired word of God and then reject the authority that declared it inspired.

Finally I could see clearly the relationship between the

authority of the Church and the value of the scriptures in my life as a Christian. How relieved I felt that, after spending so many hours and years studying and pondering this question, I finally could bring it to the point of ultimate simplicity.

19

THE GATES OF HELL
SHALL NOT PREVAIL

*W*HAT DO THE WORDS "the gates of hell shall not prevail" mean to a Christian who takes faith seriously? I know what we were all taught that they mean, but I still had to work it out for myself. People gave many answers in a cursory, casual way; it struck me as if the people had never really thought the answers out for themselves. I had to know what Jesus meant by these words.

As mentioned previously, Jesus said to Simon, "Blessed are you, Simon, son of John, because flesh and blood has not revealed this to you, but my Father in heaven. And I say to you, 'You are Rock, and on this Rock I will build my Church, and the gates of hell shall not prevail against it.' And I give to you the keys of the kingdom of heaven. Whatsoever you will bind on earth I will bind in heaven, and whatsoever you will loose on earth I will loose in heaven."

I have heard that passage interpreted to me in many different ways, to such an extent that I had to unravel it all in a way
that would make most sense to me. Jesus obviously had a mo-
tive in raising the issue of what people thought of Him. He
was not interested in the apostles relating what others thought
of Him. So, He asked them point-blank, "Who do you say
that I am?" Simon suddenly burst out with the revelation
"You are the Christ, the Son of the living God." I say "revelation" because that is what Jesus called it. His Father in heaven
revealed this to Simon. Was this a foreshadowing of how the
Spirit would work in Simon's life from then on? Jesus spoke
these words in Aramaic. William Barclay, the highly respected
Scottish Presbyterian scholar, explains it most simply. He
writes that the word Jesus used for *rock* was "cephas." "You are
Cephas, and upon this cephas I will build my Church." In
their Greek translation the words lost Jesus' play on the word.
The translation calls Simon "Petros," then has Jesus saying
"and on this petra I will build my Church." Some scholars are
now changing the words in the English translations to reflect
the Aramaic, to read: "You are Rock, and upon this rock I will
build my Church."

Barclay best explains this whole passage. After noting other
suggestions as to what Jesus meant, he concludes:

> While we agree that there is truth in these suggestions, we
> feel certain that the rock is none other than Peter himself. It
> is perfectly true that in the ultimate and eternal sense God is
> the rock on whom the Church is founded; but it is also true
> that Peter was the first man to discover and publicly to con-
> fess who Jesus was and, therefore, on him the Church is

founded. . . . Nothing can take from Peter the honor of being the first stone in the edifice of the new people of God.

Barclay then goes on to explain the meaning of the promises of Jesus to Peter:

"I will give you the keys of the kingdom of heaven." The possession of the keys always implies very special authority and power. . . . So, then Jesus is saying that Peter was to be the man who opened the door of the Kingdom, and indeed he did. At Pentecost it was the preaching of Peter which opened the door to three thousand souls (Acts 2.41). It was Peter who adventurously opened the door of the Kingdom to the Gentile centurion, Cornelius (Acts 10). It was Peter who at the Council of Jerusalem gave the decisive witness which flung open the door of the Church to the Gentiles at large (Acts 15.14).

Barclay continues:

It is then said by Jesus to Peter: "Whatever you bind on earth, shall be bound in heaven, and whatever you loose on earth will be loosed in heaven." . . . To bind something is to declare it forbidden; to loose something is to declare it allowed. In this context this is the only meaning which these two words can have. Jesus was saying to Peter: "Peter, in the days to come heavy responsibilities will be laid upon you. You, as leader of the Church, will have to make grave decisions. The guidance and direction of the young Church is going to fall on you. Will you always remember that the decisions you will be called upon to make will affect the lives and souls of men in time and eternity?" Jesus was not giving Peter some special privilege; He was giving him a grave warning of the almost unbearable responsibility that was going to be laid upon him for the welfare of the Church in the days to come.

The stability and unity that Jesus intended for His Church were not to be temporary qualities. The Church must always have what Jesus gave to Peter. The responsibilities that Peter was given to assure the Church's stability were not for just a few years but for all succeeding generations. Jesus' Church would always need Peter's guidance. Peter, as well as the other apostles, was guaranteed Jesus' wisdom and presence until the end of time. The continued presence of the Holy Spirit was also promised to Peter and the apostles when Jesus said, "I will send to you the Holy Spirit who will bring back to your minds all the things that I have taught you. . . . The Holy Spirit will teach you."

It was beginning to make sense to me. Jesus was setting His Church on a solid foundation, giving it a simple, basic structure, but one that would enable it to function for centuries to come. The heart and soul of that structure were the living presence of Jesus and the Holy Spirit to provide guidance and direction through Peter and the other apostles. Just as the scribes and Pharisees succeeded Moses, so there would always be apostles to succeed those whom Jesus had originally chosen. It seemed simple enough. The apostles were still here. Peter was still here. Why did I still have a problem?

I suppose the problem stemmed from my disappointment

and disillusionment with some of the successors of Peter and the apostles. Some were downright immoral. Recognizing that fact is difficult. I guess my question now was: What was it precisely that Jesus guaranteed to Peter and the apostles? Did He guarantee their holiness beyond reproach? There is no evidence of that, although we don't have evidence of the apostles doing anything egregiously immoral. Paul did berate Peter for being a hypocrite and following a double standard when it came to observance of the dietary laws. Then Paul was hypocritical also when, after denying that gentile Christians had to be circumcised, he went ahead and had Timothy circumcised before ordaining him a bishop. Paul also caused quite a stir when later in life he had a woman companion traveling with him; he felt annoyed enough to believe he had to defend himself against the community's gossip.

In none of the words of Jesus does He indicate that He is guaranteeing personal holiness. He is guaranteeing that the apostles and Peter will guide the Church under the Holy Spirit's protection and inspiration. He did say that the "gates of hell will never prevail against the Church," which seems to indicate a long-term struggle between the Church and Satan, but as bitter as that struggle might be, Satan will not be able to destroy the Church or trick it into teaching error.

The constant struggles in the early Church with heresy and the attempt of political rulers to dominate the Church and influence doctrine seem to fit the type of struggle with Satan that Jesus was talking about. And it looks as if that struggle will be with the Church forever. There were struggles, even in the time of the apostles, with disloyal disciples, with leaders who did not live good lives. There were many scandals even

in the churches the apostles founded. Saint Paul's many letters, especially to the Corinthians, provide graphic evidence of
that fact. The scandals were a constant heartache to him.
Some bishops who succeeded the apostles and others who followed them lived lives that were far from exemplary. It was becoming very clear that Jesus did not guarantee the holiness of
His apostles' successors. What was it He guaranteed?

That the Church would not be overcome by Satan seems
to be the key. Immorality and frightful scandal on the part of
Christians seem to be a given throughout history. As disgrace-
ful as some of the behavior has been, the Church has risen
above it and is more a beacon of hope and strength than ever,
even with the evils confronting the Church today. It seems
there will always be saints of highest holiness in the Church
alongside of the worst kind of sinners. The Church rarely
kicks out anybody, so it will always be a Church full of sinners
and, as a result, a very dysfunctional family.

I think the only area where the Church really shines is in
the sublimity and integrity of its teachings. I earlier mentioned John Trost, the artist and former editor of a Communist
newspaper in Paris. After we had become acquainted, he told
me the story of his conversion to Christianity. He told me that
he did not know which denomination had remained faithful
to Jesus' teachings as reflected in the beliefs of the earliest
Christian communities taught by the apostles. In the Columbia
University library, where he worked, he found the writings of
all the Fathers of the Church. He read them all in their original Greek and Latin and compared their teachings to the
teachings of the various modern denominations. It was only
then, after all the tedious research, that he embraced the
Catholic faith.

Departing from the teachings of the apostles and the Fathers of the Church was tantamount to departing from Christ. John Trost was convinced that the Church had remained faithful to all that the earliest Christians believed as taught to them by the apostles. The Fathers insisted on loyalty to these traditional beliefs passed on from the apostles as tests of loyalty to Jesus.

I still had a horrible problem with the frightfully un-Christian activities perpetrated by Church officials throughout history. Looking on events that happened in the later periods of the Dark Ages and more recently and realizing that Christians were still emerging from their barbarian roots were of little comfort. If Christians had really absorbed the message and spirit of Jesus, they would never have acted with such ungodly cruelty. The Christians' treatment of Jews and of Christians whom they condemned to burning at the stake as heretics is a deplorable black mark on the history of those professing to be followers of the forgiving, compassionate Jesus. Such actions they justified as necessary to protect the faith of the innocent. But this fanatical sadism and vindictiveness caused more damage to people's faith than the worst heretics. These actions were partly responsible for spawning more than one revolution on the Continent and for destroying the faith of millions of people.

Yet alongside all this evil, there was a remarkable, indeed a miraculous, phenomenon for goodness that the Church gave birth to in the darkest days of Western history. By the twelfth century the Church had already created throughout Europe dozens of universities where even poor people could be educated and become masters of higher learning. The University of Paris alone had over fifty thousand students, more students than the entire population of Paris itself at the time. There were in various cities medical colleges, as well as law and philosophy and theology colleges, and centers for science and mathematics that provided the springboard for modern science. The monasteries and universities taught and preserved classical literature and Greek and Roman philosophy. All these centers of learning were established by bishops and funded by the Church. Religious orders established orphanages and schools to educate children. Orders of nuns started schools to educate girls, which was revolutionary back in the fifteenth century. Hospitals were opened to care for the sick poor as well as for the well-to-do. New religious orders sprang up to staff these hospitals. There were also thousands of monasteries, some of strict observance, many not so strict, but all making their contribution to feed and care for the poor, providing work and shelter for them in the most difficult economic times. Besides this, art, architecture, and sculpture reached heights never before seen. The fascinating paradox that struck me was all these masterpieces of art depicted stories from the scriptures, stories Catholics were supposed to be ignorant of. And it was the Church that sponsored and encouraged this explosion of human genius that, hundreds of years later, is still the wonder of our highly technological world. Where else have we seen anything like this throughout the world? It proves Jesus right. His parable about the Church, the kingdom of heaven on earth, being like a woman who put yeast in a mass of dough, causing the dough to rise many times its size, predicted that His message would stimulate great growth throughout the whole of society where the Church exists. That is why He could refer to the Church as the pearl of great price, but also as the field where the enemy sowed weeds. Jesus had no illusions about the Church. He knew that if it was doing its job of welcoming sinners into its family, it would always have problems because of the vast numbers of sick and crippled members in the process of being saved.

And this is something many people do not realize. Some teach that a person is saved at a particular point in time. That particular point in time is when Jesus saved us by His passion, death, and Resurrection. At that point we were saved. From then on, as Saint Paul writes, "we must work out our salvation in fear and trembling." We are not saved in one moment of our own choosing. Being saved is a lifelong process of committing our lives to God and working on that commitment right up unto the end.

Whenever I think of that promise to Peter that "the gates of hell will not prevail against the Church," I get a brief glimpse into the vast vision of Jesus. In that moment of His promise, His mind transcended the whole future of the Church and saw the evil assaults of Satan's attempts to destroy the Church. His promise was, in effect, "Do not worry. All the powers of hell will never prevail against the Church. It will overcome and survive every assault of hell."

Trying to understand the Church has been very difficult for me. It is not easy to understand, and it is difficult to cope with. I suppose that is because there is no institution like it, and it is formidable in its power for good and its weakness for evil in its midst. That is why many find it so difficult to cope with. And rather than make the effort, they just walk away from it.

Interestingly, though, when people leave the Church, they cannot just leave it. When I gave talks around the world, I spent time listening quietly and patiently as former Catholics told me their stories. In my experience, when others leave one denomination and join another, they do not have the same need to justify why they made the change. Former Catholics rarely seem comfortable that they left the Church, and they seem to need a justification for their decision. I never felt I should ask them why they had to give me reasons; I had the feeling that it was as if they were making a confession, hoping that I would understand. It always left me with a feeling of sadness.

In spite of my own difficulties with the Church or, to be more precise, with difficult personalities in the Church, I had to continually condition myself to think, "They are not the Church. They are just members of the Church, and even though they may be bishops and people with important positions, I cannot allow myself to think that they are the Church." Because they stand in the place of Jesus when they teach, they can still cause much pain in the Christian community, just like the religious leaders in Jesus' day. Detaching myself from them personally so they cannot hurt me is one thing. Detaching myself from the Church would be to walk away from Jesus. That distinction became clearer as time went on. At one particular point in my life, older priests told me that if they were treated the way I was treated, they would have left the Church. That kind of thinking never made sense to me.

Although Jesus assured the Church's survival and the integrity of its transmission of His message, I had problems with the Vatican's proclamation of papal infallibility. I did not have a difficulty with Jesus promising that the Holy Spirit would guide the pope and the bishops to protect the integrity of His message. This I saw as necessary if Jesus' teaching was to survive whole and uncorrupted for the benefit of future generations of human beings searching for truth. But, since the First Vatican Council in A.D. 1870, when papal infallibility was defined, this teaching created an almost impossible wall between Christians of goodwill in other denominations and the Catholic Church. Pope John Paul II recognized this when he said a few years ago that he realized that accommodations had to be made concerning the current prerogatives of the pope and his relationship with bishops if there was to be genuine unity with bishops of other Christian churches. Many Protestant bishops, especially German Lutherans, saw this as a unique opportunity for the churches to draw closer to one another with an eye to eventual reunion. There is a great willingness on the part of many Protestant leaders to respond to Jesus' prayer for unity at the Last Supper, and this humble expression of the pope to accommodate their concerns seemed to clear the way to closer cooperation and eventual unity.

Although I accept what the Church teaches when it is solemnly defined, as well as its ordinary magisterium, I realize also that extreme pressure was put on the bishops of the First Vatican Council to approve what Pope Pius IX demanded. As a result, there will always be a cloud over that issue, which Pope John Paul II was willing to discuss with Protestant bishops. I realize that this might not now come to happen. I hope a future pope will make that issue a priority; the time seems ripe for Christians of goodwill to come together to heal wounds in Jesus' family, wounds that have been a scandal for so many centuries.

When I gave talks around the country, I saw how Protestants are willing to accept what I said about Jesus and His teachings, even teachings that were uniquely Catholic. On every occasion without exception they would come up to have books signed afterward and tell me that they would join my church if I had a parish in their area. It made me realize how simple unity can be. On a number of occasions they even suggested during a question-and-answer period that I start my own church. "Don't you realize you would start out with hundreds of thousands of Joshua fans from all different denominations who would follow you?"

That suggestion, however, did not please me. Rather, I felt disappointed because I realized they had missed the point of my message. I responded as gently as I could, so as not to offend them, that I would feel very guilty if I started my own religion. Only God can tell us how He wants us to worship Him, and I would feel guilty of terrible disloyalty if I left the religion Jesus gave us and started my own. It is our responsibility to make our own feeble attempts to encourage religious leaders to be more faithful to the spirit of the Good Shepherd in the way they view themselves and in the way they treat people. But, as far as starting my own religion, such things are offensive to Jesus because it further tears apart His family, and confuses non-Christians as to what Jesus is all about and whether it is possible to find the authentic teachings of Jesus when there is so much confusion even among Christians.

20

THE CHURCH
AND DEMOCRACY

AN ISSUE THAT BAFFLED ME for a long time was: What
are the rights of the Church within a democratic form of government? What are the obligations of the Church in a democracy? Can the Church rest comfortably in a democratic
society, or will there of necessity always be tension? This is a
particular problem in our own country. The Catholic Church
is certain that its authority comes from God. In ages past, especially when people and the Church believed in the divine
right of kings, it was assumed that the king also received his
authority from God. Since both the Church and the state had
their authority from God, it was the obligation of the state to
protect the Church and for the Church to respect the authority of the kings. Which authority superseded the other was
cause for mortal struggle between the two for centuries.

Since the Second Vatican Council, A.D. 1962–65, the issue

has to a great extent been solved for the Catholic Church. The Church is very much aware that its authority has come directly from Jesus. It also recognizes that the authority of the state comes from the people, though the inalienable rights of the people come from God. The state then has no obligation to advance any particular religion. This newfound doctrine is finding its first test in the United States because of the country's unique and confusing constitutional structure. The founding fathers recognized God as Creator and the source of our inalienable and fundamental human rights, particularly the right of freedom and the right to choose our own form of government. They felt comfortable, however, even as elected officials, to lead the citizens in prayer at critical times, in recognition of our dependence on God.

However, when they defined the structure of government and laid down the rights of the citizenry, they left to the people themselves the right to fashion their own code of laws and ethics and stated in the Constitution that the state would make no laws establishing a national religion. The framers of the Constitution may have meant merely that the government could not choose any particular religion or religious denomination as the established religion of the nation. The implication was that all religions were to be extended equal respect. In the course of time this has come to mean that God Himself was to be ostracized from public life; that the divine law, as the framers of the Constitution knew it, was to be isolated from public life; and that the moral beliefs of any particular religion were not to be reflected in the laws of the land. Laws, including those concerning moral issues, were to be determined not by God's law or by the laws of any particular religion, but by the will of the people. God's laws, the Ten Commandments, the laws of any religion, were rendered irrelevant in the process of determining the law of the land. The people were to decide on their own the code of morality for the country. It does not seem that this is what the founding fathers intended, but this is the way the courts, even the Supreme Court, now interprets the Constitution.

It is one thing not to show favoritism to any particular religion, but it is an entirely different thing to banish God from the public life of the nation. There is no justification for that in the Constitution. I doubt if the framers of the Constitution intended to establish a godless society. Someday in the not-too-distant future we as a nation, seeing signs that threaten our place on the world stage, we will feel a need to plead with God to come to our aid. And then no one will be embarrassed or ashamed to fall on their knees and beg for God's help.

I will never forget an incident that took place in an airport terminal one evening when a number of us were desperately hoping we could get to our destination. I had been waiting since early morning with Sister Dorothy for our flight to take off for Florida. Early the next morning we were supposed to attend the open house for Café Joshua, a classy new restaurant for the homeless. A rather large, stately man came walking toward the gate area, commenting aloud to no one in particular about waiting all day. I said hello and asked if he was waiting for the flight to Palm Beach. He was. We introduced ourselves, and I said, "Oh, Shalom Koplowitz? I know you. You are one of my brother Ed's dearest friends."

"I know you then. You're the priest, that famous author,"

he replied, half in jest, then continued, "Well, you'd better pray our plane gets here, or we're all going to be in big trouble."

I laughed and said, "You're the one who should be praying. You're a blood relative of Jesus."

"Yes, but we need a minyan of at least ten men to pray. All you need is two or three gathered in His name," Shalom countered, reflecting Jesus' promise. Then in his big, booming voice he called out to the other five or six people waiting, "Are you all waiting for this flight?"

When they said yes, he called them over to pray.

One man said, "I am a Jew and I never prayed before."

"Well, I'm a Jew too, and I pray. It's about time you started," Shalom shot back good-naturedly.

Another man said he was a Baptist, and he'd be glad to pray with us. A lady came over and said, "I'm a Muslim, and I'd be honored to pray with you all."

Still another man came over and said, "I never prayed in my life, but if it will help, I'll pray with you."

In that little group there were a nun, two Jews, a Baptist, a nonbeliever, a Muslim, and a priest. We all held hands and Shalom prayed, since he was a blood relative. We all said a loud amen at the end.

No sooner had we finished than the lady agent at the desk called over to us, "Well, this is the quickest answer I have ever witnessed to a prayer. They just called from Pittsburgh, and the plane is taking off. It should be here in less than an hour."

The ones who never prayed before said, "That's the first time I prayed, and it really works. I'll have to do this more often." They were not the slightest bit embarrassed.

The abortion issue, the issue of prayer in the schools, and others have thrown the country's religious establishment into a frenzy of fear that God might someday be totally banished from public life, just to avoid hurting people's feelings. Even those denominations that were fearful of the Catholic Church attaining ascendancy in the country now find themselves struggling to control the decision-making machinery of government in a frantic attempt to preserve God's law as the law of the land. The Supreme Court decision in *Roe v. Wade* was the issue that lit the fuse for this religious explosion in the country. Other issues are now adding fuel to what could become a constitutional crisis. For over two hundred years a religious crisis over the Constitution was hardly ever a problem, other than during the "Monkey trial" over the teaching of evolution in the schools. Of late, it is not only one problem. It is a chain of problems fast running out of control. If it continues, we will subtly be working our way back to a theocracy, as radical religious leaders clearly do not feel comfortable with the democratic process and want judges who will do their bidding. This is frightening.

It is not just the fundamentalists among the Baptists and those religions loosely related to them; fundamentalists of other denominations are entering the fray. A majority of the people are concerned, with huge numbers wanting to hold on to the traditional morality of their parents and ancestors. Few are ready for a radical departure from the Ten Commandments and the moral mandates of the "Old-Time Religion." It has not yet reached the point of going to war, but there have already been fatalities in the struggle. I am afraid that feelings are running so strong and so deep that eventually there is going to be more violence. If deeply religious people feel that everything they were taught as sacred is being threatened by people who do not share their belief in God and who insist on pressuring the courts to cut God out of public life, radicals among them may resort to frightening actions.

The reason underlying these constitutional issues is that we never realized what a "democratic republic" means. It means that people determine their own way of life and the culture and morality of the nation. The possibilities for cultural upheaval are staggering, as a free people question and test the pillars of the traditional values. If our way of life is to survive, we have to work out an entirely new way to make our feelings and convictions felt concerning the direction of our country. And it cannot be the churches that do this. That is part of the problem today. Clergy are pressuring their parishioners on how to vote and what to vote for and even whom to vote for. Clergy are also using their influence to pressure the legislatures to craft laws that reflect the religious beliefs of their denominations. This is happening because, deep down, the churches do not feel comfortable in a democracy, and they are beginning to use strong-arm tactics to assure observance of their moral teachings. They fail to realize that in a democracy denominational religious laws are not, nor should they ever be, a consideration in the framing of laws. It has to be what the people themselves decide they want, not what the clergy tell them they must want. That kind of tactic will backfire in our society. If we want a country with a stable moral system, we as clergy are going to have to learn new ways of teaching our people: not just telling them what to believe but explaining to them why we believe what we believe and why certain things are right and why certain things are wrong. We can't just say that "It is part of the religion." Concerned persons have to go into the political arena and, when defending an issue or opposing an issue, not use as an argument that this is part of our religion, but that this issue is good for our country for these reasons or bad for our country for these reasons. If the people are well informed by their clergy, who themselves have taken time to give reasons to people and not just dictate morality, then we have a chance to survive as a strong nation with solid moral values.

This is not going to be easy, because all too often we as clergy have not explained things to our people. We have just told them that this is what we believe and we have to accept it because it is part of our religion. We have to develop the practice of explaining to people why we believe what we do; otherwise we will continue to treat them as children who are not allowed to do their own thinking. People must rise to the occasion and come to the defense of what they themselves believe, not what the churches tell them to believe. As Saint Peter wrote in his letter: "Find a reason for your faith."

The Church's involvement in the present constitutional crisis has troubled me greatly. The abortion issue is one we can hardly talk about rationally because too many radical people on both sides have used hateful confrontational tactics when defending their positions. When I was a pastor, I tried to share with the congregation my own struggle with the issue. After Mass, even people in favor of abortion came over to me and said, "Father, you're shrewd. You know you don't really have a struggle with abortion, but what you said made me do a lot of soul-searching. It was a big help. Thanks." I just smiled.

Our people need sermons explaining the important human issues of our times. In days past, bishops, as the official teachers of the people, used to give beautiful expositions of faith and discussed critical issues with their people in a way they could understand. This is more critical now than ever, since our people's involvement in the formulation of laws demands an in-depth knowledge of all the issues that are at stake.

We, as clergy and laypeople, have not handled the abortion issue in a prudent and effective way. The way we go about it does not win friends. It has heated up the controversy to the point where no one listens, and more and more noise is generated. We cannot assume that those who do not see things our way are evil and accuse them of things they do not understand.

I have found that many people of goodwill do not share our Catholic belief that God creates a soul for each embryo that is beginning to grow. Even our own belief that God creates a soul at conception is not something that the Church has always taught. There were continual controversies over this issue for many years. It is not hard to see how people who have not been brought up in our faith can have a wide variety of ideas as to when a fetus becomes a human being. It is difficult to accuse them of evil when they do not share our belief that an embryo is an immortal being that has already received a soul from God. Also, many people have no concept of a spiritual soul. It is much wiser for us to sit down and become acquainted with their thinking and why they think that way, and then share our thoughts with them so we can at least understand each other, even if we cannot come to a meeting of

minds. I cannot understand why we have to have fierce public conflicts because we disagree. It is much wiser to calmly
discuss our differences with people than to accuse them of evil
and incite anger and meanness and lose support of many un-
decided people of goodwill because of our own mean spirit.
And when it comes to the making of laws, it is important to
win friends and at least have the goodwill of those who are un-
decided and are still considering the issue. There is nothing
more offensive or self-defeating than self-righteousness in
public discussions. I have had more success with people who
favor abortion by being patient and courteous in my attempt
to understand their position. They appreciated my willingness
to listen. They then felt obliged to understand where I was
coming from, and they began to appreciate my position on
the issue, even if they could not adopt it for themselves.
Becoming friends even brought us closer in other ways, and I
was surprised to see them coming to church occasionally, especially when they were not of our faith.

I think what troubles me most, however, is that many of us
as clergy have not done a good job of instilling strong moral
values in our people. Feeling we have failed when it comes to
the abortion issue, we then decide to pressure the legislators
by various means to enact laws forcing people to do what we
have failed to inspire them to do. That is not the way things
should work in a democracy. It makes me feel sometimes that
we do not understand the democratic process or, understanding it, do not feel comfortable living within its framework.

In these critical times we as clergy have a great responsibility to defend our moral values and explain to our people the
underlying reasons for our beliefs and for our way of life. We

are going to have to give them more than just a fifteen-minute sermon on a Sunday morning, together with a pious commentary on scripture. We have to become what the early Fathers of the Church were forced to become, Christian philosophers, competing with the unhealthy philosophies trying to soften the moral fiber of our society. We must delve deeply into our theology and philosophy, which we looked on as unneeded for ministry, and learn to make our tried and solidly grounded philosophical system applicable to the critical circumstances in which we live. We have to be able to explain to our people what is good for our society and what is detrimental to our way of life in our country and also why some ethical decision is good or bad.

Another aspect of the abortion issue which troubles me deeply is the practice of some bishops who try to excommunicate or penalize Catholic candidates for public office who are opposed to abortion but will accept the Supreme Court decision on the issue. It bothers me because it shows that those bishops do not believe in the democratic process, or do not understand that in the type of government that we have, the people have the right to decide on many moral issues. If there are people who believe that an embryo does not have a soul like we believe, and is not a person until a certain level of development, we cannot insist that they are wrong and we are right, and that our belief become the law of the land. There are even other Christians who do not believe what we believe on when human life begins. Therefore, we cannot offhandedly accuse them of approving of murder if they approve of abortion, especially since we as Catholics cannot prove scientifically that we are right and that the others are wrong. I find it impossible to understand, however, how people can see a fully developed fetus full of life in an ultrasound image, and can honestly say it is not human, and in conscience kill it. At that point, it is so obvious, I don't know how the Supreme Court can approve of such an abortion.

When it comes to the issue of candidates for public office, since we live in a democracy, Catholic candidates can be, in good conscience, personally opposed to abortion and still defend the government's right to legislate differently from what we believe. That is just how democracy works.

I can appreciate the Church's responsibility not just to preach to its own members but to be a witness of God to the whole world. In doing this the Church has the obligation to set before people the highest and noblest of ideals. In attempting to do this the Vatican has its representatives present in many world bodies, such as the United Nations. Its representatives there take notably strong positions on moral issues. At times, however, I feel they step over the line of prudence when they insist that the international body observe the Catholic Church's unique view on certain matters, especially when those views are not even universally accepted by theologians within the Church. I can understand their strong antiabortion stand, but actively and strongly opposing the United Nations' advice to use condoms as one of various means of reducing the spread of the HIV virus and AIDS does not seem to make good sense, and makes the Vatican look irrelevant in its response to serious humanitarian crises.

21

JESUS: A PROBLEM FOR THE CHURCHES?

W HEN SIMEON PROPHESIED in the temple on the occasion of Jesus' Presentation that the child was destined to influence the rise and fall of many in Israel and would be a sign of contradiction, Simeon was referring primarily to the people of his time. However, lately I am becoming more and more aware that the prophecy is as valid today in Christianity as it was in Judaism in Simeon's time: This child is still a sign of contradiction, and a stumbling block. No one even calls Him Jesus, which is His name. They pray to Christ, refer to Him as Christ; they talk and write about Christ as if they don't know His real name. It is almost as if we don't relate to Him on an intimate basis. We call Him by His title. How odd!

I guess I had always assumed that Jesus was the primary focus of Christians' lives, especially the lives of religious leaders. Only in my later years did I come to the shocking realization that Jesus can be quite irrelevant in the life of the churches: not just in a few churches, but really, I feel, perhaps most churches. This was first driven home to me one day when an old priest, who had been a friend all my life, said to me, "How can you talk about Jesus for an hour and a half?"

I was stunned. I asked him what he meant by that. His response was "We were not taught about Jesus in the seminary. We had good scripture courses, and excellent courses in moral and dogmatic theology and in Christology, and all the other courses, but we weren't taught anything about the personal aspects of Jesus' life. I don't think I could talk about Him for more than five minutes. Oh, I can talk about passages in the gospels and draw lessons from them, but that's it."

Not long after that some of my Protestant minister friends told me the same thing. Soon I became obsessed with the issue and asked the same question of a good number of the clergy, with pretty much the same response, though some became defensive and said rather sheepishly that they learned a lot about Jesus from their course in the New Testament. I also had had a good course in the New Testament, and I know you really don't get a very profound picture of Jesus in studying the New Testament. It's an exercise in exegesis. A number of scripture professors in various denominations told me that they had never met a real flesh-and-blood Jesus until they read *Joshua*, the first book I had written. One very well-known priest, who had been scripture advisor to Pope Paul VI, told me he had read *Joshua* fifteen times because it ministered to him in ways nothing else ever did.

Just because people talk about Jesus and say we should get to know Jesus does not mean we ever get around to learning more about Him. Try to have a conversation about Jesus with some good religious friends. You will be surprised how soon someone changes the subject. Christians are very unfamiliar with Jesus' life and how He really feels and thinks about issues. We may say He is compassionate and forgiving and merciful, but it ends there. And clergy are no different. It is surprising how little clergymen know about Jesus. It was a most welcome surprise to come across a parish every now and then that made Jesus the focus of parish life, by having the people, with the pastor's guidance, ask, "How would Jesus want us to treat this person, these kinds of people, or to handle this situation?" That is the way parishes should be run. It is rare, but it is beautiful when you do see it.

Last year I sent a letter to all the cardinals, archbishops, and bishops, telling them of my experiences over the past twenty years of speaking tours and explaining how many priests and ministers told me that they were never taught about Jesus in the seminary, other than in Christology courses and whatever they may have picked up in studying the gospels or from personal spiritual direction. I received some beautiful responses from some bishops and cardinals, saying that they would do what they could to promote establishing courses about the personal life of Jesus in seminaries, but most bishops were defensive, telling me that they already have good programs built into the schedule to familiarize the seminarians with a deep knowledge of Jesus. I guess they wanted to show me that I must be misinformed. All their letters did, however, was convince me of the great value they placed on programs we all know to be shallow. They also convinced me that they really did not care whether seminarians had an intimate knowledge of the personal life of Jesus. If seminarians were taught about Jesus in an intimate, personal way, there would not be so many young scribes and Pharisees in parishes today treating people with the same callous insensitivity as their forefathers in the Jewish religion. It is as if they had never heard of the Good Shepherd, who endlessly sought out the lost, the troubled, the bruised and hurting sheep excommunicated by the Pharisees, and, placing them on His shoulders, carried them back home.

Responses from college deans were more to the point. They said that courses about Jesus were not academic, and so teaching about Jesus would not have a proper place in a college curriculum. Courses about Mohammed and Buddha, what their lives were like, and what was an authentic way of understanding their teachings, could be academic. So, I asked myself: What then is the purpose of a Christian college if the students cannot develop an intimate understanding of the founder of their religion? Are we ashamed of Jesus? Is He too simple for a highly intellectual professor to spend time making Him real to students hungry to learn about Him? People of all denominations have so often told me that they rarely hear a sermon about the personal life and feelings of Jesus. Why is He so thoroughly ostracized from our schools and our pulpits? Where are Christians expected to go to learn about Jesus?

Some will answer glibly, "Read the gospels. That's all anyone needs. They are inspired by the Holy Spirit." Why then have scripture scholars told me that they had analyzed the scriptures all their lives and never got to know Jesus?

Surely there must be some clergy and scholars who have

not just analyzed the gospels but studied and pondered them in prayer in an effort to get to know Jesus and His personal life, His feelings, His beliefs, His attitudes about so many thousands of issues, and in the process become so familiar with Him that they can touch the hearts of others, especially the young, who desperately need to know Him.

This is one painful problem I have with the churches: As an elderly lady in Elyria, Ohio, said to me one night, "Father, the way I size up Christianity is like this: The Catholics worship the Church, the Protestants worship the Bible, and there are darn few who ever get to know Jesus Christ." She was right, and it is tragic.

22

ECUMENISM

i ALWAYS FELT THAT UNITY among the churches should be easy. I still feel that way. It is so significant that at the Last Supper, when the small community of Jesus' followers were so closely bound together with Him, He should pray openly to His Father for unity among His followers. It was as if His vision transcended time and He foresaw a terrible cataclysm in the Church, a cataclysm that would not heal His Church but would scandalize the world for centuries. It was as if He were pleading with His Heavenly Father to prevent it so that the Church could present to the pagan world a powerful vision of unity as proof of God's presence in the Church: "Even as you have sent me into the world, so I also have sent them into the world. And for them I sanctify myself, that they also may be sanctified in truth. Yet, not for these only do I pray, but for those also who through their word are to believe in me, that all may be one even as you and I are one, that they also may be one in us so that the world may believe that you have sent me."

I always felt that Jesus' prayer for unity placed an obligation of loyalty on each of us, His followers, to make our little contribution to reestablish that unity. When I became a pastor, a local Lutheran pastor, Don Marxhausen, and I became good friends. We were both busy, so we did not socialize much, but we did church things together, which brought our two parishes very close. We realized that both our peoples believed much the same things, and both had pretty much the same ideas about the Bishop of Rome as the successor of Peter and having whatever Jesus gave to Peter. We even had joint services. While we stood at the same altar, he consecrated what he had placed on the altar and later distributed that to his parishioners, while I distributed what I had consecrated to my parishioners. We also developed a joint creed, which both our congregations recited together. I cannot tell you the joy this gave to all of us. We even talked both of our bishops into being willing to co-confirm the young people in our parishes. From that point on it was just a matter of fine-tuning what we all should believe as loyal followers of Jesus and what He would be expecting of us.

We did have one snag, however, and it was more humorous than tragic. The feast of Our Lady of Mount Carmel, the name of our parish, was approaching. We usually had a nine-day series of prayers and sermons in preparation, then a big celebration on the night of the feast itself. In an Italian parish, celebrations are big operations, and more fun than you can imagine. Well, with tongue in my cheek, I asked Don if he would be willing to give a sermon about Mary on one of the evenings. His response was volcanic: "Girzone, you're pushing my ecumenism way past the limit. Lutherans don't have anything to do with her."

I responded, "Well, you don't know much about Martin Luther, I guess."

"What do you mean by that remark?"

"Nothing other than Martin Luther used to give beautiful sermons about Mary, which apparently well-informed Lutheran pastors don't know much about."

"Girzone, I don't know how we ever became friends. I'll do my research and if you're right, we'll talk about it."

At two o'clock in the morning my phone rang. Coming out of a deep sleep, I tried to be gracious. "Hello!"

"Well, if I can't sleep, you're not going to sleep either." It was the German shepherd.

"What's troubling you now, big bear?"

"I'm just lying here in bed, wide awake, reading Luther's sermons on Mary. They're beautiful."

"Interesting you had to learn about that from a Roman priest."

"I'm happy that even you are learning from Luther. You know, as I'm reading this sermon, I can see how this would be a great sermon to give in your church. I'd be glad to do it, so count me in. And I can tell all my friends that Luther is finally being preached in a Catholic Church."

"Great, but don't forget to add that only a Catholic church would allow it. Try to preach it in your church."

"Girzone, you can be a big pain in the lower back, but I still love you."

"The feeling's mutual. Go on to sleep. I'll talk to you to-morrow."

Pastor Marxhausen's sermon was a most memorable event. Our people were thrilled at the beautiful words the Lutheran pastor read from Martin Luther's sermon on Mary. I think it was probably the first time any church in the United States, Catholic or Lutheran, had heard Luther's words about the Blessed Virgin preached. My parishioners were not only surprised but inspired by that remarkably tender sermon, read with such sensitivity.

It wasn't just the Lutheran parish our people teamed up with. We also had an extraordinary relationship with the Orthodox Jewish community. The State of New York had taken over the local synagogue to build a highway through the city. However, the amount of compensation the state gave the Jewish community was not enough to rebuild the synagogue. I brought that up at the next parish council meeting. After discussing the matter, the council decided unanimously to write to the rabbi and offer to start a fund-raising drive to rebuild the synagogue.

The Jewish community was overwhelmed that a Catholic parish would offer to do such a thing. While the fund-raising drive turned out not to be needed, our two communities became best of friends and did wonderful things together. The rabbi, Sam Bloom, and I became dear friends. When the new temple was built, I was asked to speak. I can't tell you what an honor it was for me to speak on such an occasion at an Orthodox synagogue. I had so many things to share with our Jewish friends that afternoon.

I told them that our two communities had grown so close over the past few years, it made me think about many things that could be possible that might seem impossible to many people. I had been thinking how the earliest Christian communities were Jewish. Even though they accepted Jesus as the Messiah, they still were faithful to Judaism, attending temple services regularly and meeting on Sunday evenings for their Christian Eucharist service. The apostles themselves did the same thing, and they saw nothing contradictory about what they were doing. So I asked myself, "Why not today?" I then made the proposal: "I would love to see the day when I could join your temple and still be the pastor of Our Lady of Mount Carmel parish, and when whoever among your people may in their hearts believe that Jesus is the Messiah could become a member of our parish and still remain a loyal member of your temple."

I was surprised at the applause. Two Orthodox rabbis came up to me afterward and said, "What a remarkable suggestion! We see no reason why it cannot work."

It was not just a hairbrained idea that crossed my mind. It was a well-thought-out concept that developed over a period of years, starting when I used to bring my students to a synagogue in Pottsville, Pennsylvania, on Friday nights so they could experience what Jesus experienced when He attended the local synagogue services while growing up.

I asked my bishop if I could join a synagogue and still be pastor. He said he would have to think about it. Not hearing from him, I decided to write a paper describing the whole idea and sent it to the apostolic delegate in Washington. He responded very positively to the concept and sent the paper to the Catholic bishops' liaison office that works with the Jewish community. A short time later we corresponded. I was told that, while it was a novel idea, they could see nothing wrong with it, and it might be a good start in forming a bond with the Jewish community. Unfortunately, a short time later my parish and another parish were merged and the pastors were asked to resign, so a new pastor could be appointed to serve both parishes. Also, my rabbi friend's wife died, and shortly after, the rabbi himself died. Unfortunately, nothing came of the dream, but the possibility is still there for some priest who might be inclined to work out the details with some rabbi and his or her community.

These events showed me how simple and workable unity can be where there are people of goodwill and brave hearts willing to take the steps necessary to respond to Jesus' heartfelt prayer for unity at the Last Supper. I always felt that if we waited for theologians to work out acceptable formulas for belief, unity would take forever. That approach assumes that people of a whole denomination will automatically believe what the theologians have decided. From experience, when I gave talks to large mixed crowds from all denominations, the people were very open to everything I presented. In fact, one person said at a talk, "Father, if you start your own church, we will all join it." Everyone clapped. I told them I could not do something like that. I would feel disloyal to Jesus. He gave us our religion. It is our responsibility to help make the Church faithful to His dreams, not break it up by starting new churches. They understood that. But I see ecumenism as workable only if we use the approach that I know works from my own personal experience. I hope the clergy and bishops will seriously consider this model, even if with different and more creative modifications, as a practical way to make unity a reality.

23

CONFESSION:
THE SACRAMENT OF PEACE

i WROTE EARLIER ABOUT THE APOSTLES slowly becoming aware that Jesus had given them the power to forgive
sin and reconcile sheep who had fallen away from the community. As time went on, however, the practice of reconciliation changed. Public confession of sins and public penance
were not the only means of reconciliation. Early documents
list ten ways of reconciling with God: among them are almsgiving, expressing sorrow for sin, penance, charitable works,
private confession of sins to a priest, and public confession before the community.

Much later on monks with very rigid sensitivity to personal guilt thought that the only way people could worthily
receive the Eucharist was if they made frequent confession of
sins to a priest. All mortal sins had to be confessed before a
person could receive the Eucharist. Often people had a diffi-

cult time distinguishing between mortal sins and other sins, which introduced much confusion in sensitive souls, and bred scrupulosity and extreme anxiety among people. Confession for some people became a nightmare, especially when they could not remember whether they had confessed a particular sin and the number of times they had committed that sin. They would then worry as to whether they received Communion unworthily.

These problems are particularly troubling to elderly people who realize they are approaching their last days and dread going before God with unconfessed or unrepented sins. At the time in their lives when they should be comforted by thoughts of a loving, forgiving God, they waste time dreading their meeting with a punishing Judge.

Of course, there are some people who do not have sensitive consciences, and confession may be of little or no concern in their life, which is not good either. They miss the wonderful opportunity to bring God's healing love and forgiveness into their souls by confessing those sins to a priest, expressing sorrow for their sins, and being assured of God's forgiveness. The therapy that flows from confession is like a healing balm for the soul that has done evil things to a neighbor or seriously offended against the goodness of a loving God.

I struggled with the idea of confession for a long time. When, years ago, we used to hear twelve hundred children's confessions each month, I felt they were not really beneficial. The children would confess the same sins month after month. You knew they did it only because it was part of the schedule. I sometimes heard children outside the confessional asking friends what they were going to tell the priest. I knew they were making up their confessions and that what they were confessing was not real.

I always felt that confession is a special gift of Jesus designed to bring healing to troubled souls with genuine sins on their consciences. I knew from experience the peace that confession can bring to someone who is particularly troubled. Some of the most healing confessions I have heard were at an airport terminal or when meeting a parishioner walking down the street. Once I had brought a group of biology students to the New York Museum of Natural History. Afterward, as we sat having pizza and Cokes for lunch, a man approached me and asked if I would hear his confession. That was an inspired moment and a really beautiful experience. It was natural and not on schedule, and came from the man's heart. That was the way Jesus intended confession and reconciliation to take place.

When it is used the way Jesus intended, confession can be a vehicle for peace and serenity for so many people. When Jesus first introduced it to the apostles, the words He used give us the key: "Peace be with you. Receive the Holy Spirit. Whose sins you shall forgive, they are forgiven them. . . ." Confession was intended as a peace-bearing gift to troubled souls. And I have found it to be just that.

I will never forget a phone call I received a couple of years ago. A lady called me from far away. She told me she had just read my book *Joshua,* and it moved her deeply. She told me she was a great sinner, not the kind that everybody says they are. "I am a real sinner. I don't think there is a sin I did not commit. After I read *Joshua* I wanted to make my peace with God, but I was afraid of confessing to a holy priest, for fear I might shock him so much he might refuse me absolution. So I asked a friend of mine if she knew a priest who was a sinner. She told me she did. I went to him, and as I told him my confession, the grace that poured from that priest's soul washed over my whole being and brought me a peace and closeness to God I had never dreamed was possible." She ended by saying, "Thank God for sinful priests. They understand." I could repeat that experience a thousand times. I don't think people realize the therapeutic value of confession. Many psychiatrists do. Even those who are not Christian have often said to me how confession to a priest has brought such peace and healing to their patients.

It is particularly healing and comforting for people on the verge of dying who are afraid of meeting God because, at that time in their lives, they are so acutely aware of so many things they have done wrong. To share them with a priest who they feel confident has the power to reconcile them with God has a most comforting effect on a person's soul. The priest can see the effect immediately, as the person settles into a peaceful tranquility that has clearly banished the fear of meeting God.

24

CELIBACY: MANDATORY OR OPTIONAL?

CELIBACY IS ONE of the hotly debated issues in the Church today. It is something every priest has to struggle with during his whole life. For some it is more of a struggle than it is for others, but it is a cause for the deepest concern because so many priests' lives have been severely damaged or ruined by this inner conflict.

Some men can live celibate lives with relative ease, especially if they are not of a deeply emotional nature. Some enjoy living alone. Some, possessed of a profound need for privacy, can more easily accept celibacy. Others, who may have a strong need to share their life with someone else, often find celibacy a terrifying experience and a dangerous psychological trap that can lead to debilitating chronic depression. I have known priests to whom this has happened, and the depression sometimes led them to consider suicide. When I tried to discuss this with clergy or laypeople who could not imagine the pain of these priests, they would callously retort, "They made their vows like everybody else. Let them keep them. It is not easy for married people to keep their vows, so why should we feel sympathy for priests who have problems?" I could never understand their callous insensitivity or their inability to understand the difference.

Over the years, knowing priests who were having this problem and fighting the concomitant depression, I tried to understand why the issue could not be resolved. Reading the gospels one day, the words of Jesus struck me: "There are some who are celibate by nature; there are some who are celibate by choice; there are some who are celibate for the sake of the kingdom. Let him who can take it, take it." It dawned on me for the first time that Jesus made celibacy optional and hinted that there are some who cannot take it, meaning that God may not have given them the grace to live a celibate life.

The call to celibacy is a gift of God's grace. If God has called a person to celibacy, that is a beautiful gift. The call to the priesthood is also a beautiful gift of grace. Besides being a responsibility, it is also a privilege. If God calls a person to the priesthood and gives him the call to celibacy with the corresponding grace necessary to live a celibate life, that is an extraordinary witness to God. If, however, God calls a person to the priesthood and does not give him the call to celibacy with the grace necessary to observe it, for the Church to demand it can destroy an otherwise good priest, as has happened so often through the centuries. Not to see what is so obvious is being blind to the work of the Holy Spirit in a person's life. A sensitive, caring bishop should be the first one to recognize that a priest has a genuine call to the priesthood and not a call to celibacy, and make the decisions necessary to assure the priest's integrity and holiness of life, which might mean taking a strong stand with other bishops to reevaluate long-standing Church regulations. "Consider the Sabbath was made for man and not man for the Sabbath." The law was made for man, not man for the law. Where there is a serious human need, the law must bend. Where serious damage is occasioned by a law, the law must be changed. A law that brings about the destruction of God's children is never a good law. When a law causes the destruction of the priesthood and deprives millions of God's people of Mass and the Eucharist, the hierarchy cannot afford to ignore what could possibly be prodding from the Holy Spirit, without falling liable to Jesus' accusation against the Pharisees: "You make void the law of God for mere human traditions."

Churches are closing. Many people have difficulty finding a church where the Eucharist is celebrated by priests. Old folks find it almost impossible to find a place to worship. Priests are overworked to the point where it can only serve to shorten their lives, as more and more responsibilities are laid on them at a time in their lives when responsibilities should be lightened, not weighted more heavily on them. The sin is that nothing is being done to respond to the needs of the people. I know it is not cowardice that prevents bishops from speaking out and forcing change. I know they really care about their people's need for Mass and the Eucharist. I know it is not fear of censure or of losing a promotion that paralyzes them from taking a bold stand. I know they realize that there are hundreds of thousands of faithful people who are being deprived of the Eucharist and the sacraments in hospitals, prisons, and nursing homes. What I cannot understand is why they are doing nothing to provide priests for our people. I cannot believe that the Holy Spirit is not calling people to the priesthood. Maybe we are rejecting many whom the Holy Spirit is calling.

Many priests who have left the priesthood to marry were considered by others who worked with them as holy, prayerful, dedicated priests; clearly they could not live a celibate life. Does that not indicate that the Holy Spirit gave them the call to the priesthood but did not give them the call to celibacy? A sensitive, caring hierarchy should be the first to recognize that something is wrong. It is estimated that as many as fifty thousand priests may have left, many because they could not live alone. And we witness the strange paradox of the Church allowing married Protestant ministers to come into the Church and continue carrying out their priestly ministry, while still keeping out the vast numbers of former Catholic priests who would be only too willing to come back and work again as priests. That is hard to understand, especially when in so many places our people are spiritually starving for Jesus' sacred banquet.

It is hard for me to understand why the advice of Saint Paul about choosing a bishop has not been taken seriously. Paul said: "If one wants to become a bishop, I suppose it is a good aspiration. But let him be a man of tried and proven virtue, married only once." If the hierarchy had taken Saint Paul's counsel seriously, imagine how it could have affected the history of Christianity. It is not that celibacy could not be an option; celibacy is a blessed gift of God, and draws the priest into an even more intimate identification with Jesus. For that reason there will always be celibate priests, totally focused on their ministry of bringing Jesus to the world. But celibacy is a special calling that, when given, enhances the priesthood. If God does not give the calling to one whom He has called to the priesthood, the hierarchy must respect the Holy Spirit's choice and not say the Holy Spirit made a mistake. The scandalous refusal to provide priests for vast numbers of people is a powerful indication that we are rejecting persons whom the Spirit has called to the priesthood. This is an issue that must be faced and resolved out of fidelity to God and a sense of responsibility to the Christian people.

25

DEATH AND DYING

MANY OF THE SAINTS, beginning with Saint Paul, said they looked forward with joy to leaving this world and the chance to be with God. Was there no fear, no anxiety, no sense of terror at the prospect of leaving loved ones, and the grief it would cause them? I find that hard to imagine.

When I was younger, I used to long for the time when I could be with God. At the time, I was far from that prospect ever happening. Now that I am older, much older, and I lie in bed at night and notice my heart not beating the way it should, I am daily faced with the prospect of dying. And I have to admit, I am frightened. The thought of leaving loved ones and those who need us is a horrible experience. The realization I could have done much more than I did with my life and ministry humbles me. As memory fades, it is the good things that seem to fade, but our sins and mistakes of the past and things we should have done but did not do are vivid. We cry at the realization of how weak and selfish we have been. Though we pray continually for those we have hurt or could have helped but did not help for some reason or other, the thought of our inadequacy is painful. The prospect of meeting God is no longer the happy dream it once was. There is a strong feeling of dread as we become conscious of our unworthiness to be invited to come and live with God and our saintly loved ones, who are already there waiting for us. Some people may throw up a glib remark: "If you had faith in the Lord Jesus as your Lord and Savior, you would know you were saved." That kind of thinking does not reflect a very deep spirituality. It is the way a person feels who has just recently found the Lord. It was the way I felt and believed when I was younger. When you grow older and are faced with the near prospect of death, it is not that easy. Saint Paul may have wished he could be dissolved from this life and be with Christ, but it was probably when he was older that he made this remark: "We must work out our salvation in fear and trembling." That sounds like the mature thought of an older person, more conscious of the realities of life and the finality of death in its severing of all earthly bonds and the proximity of appearing before the judgment seat of the all-holy God.

Being faced with the prospect of the nearness of death forces us to enter into our intimacy with God and seek a more mature understanding of what He expects of us at this time in our life and how He wants us to feel about our dissolution from this life. Some people are filled with terror, some with a certain peacefulness. Nevertheless, it seems that everyone—even very holy people—has a certain amount of concern about dying. I was not surprised when a close associate of the late Pope John Paul II, when asked if the pope had been afraid of dying, responded, "Yes, as holy as he was, and as committed to Jesus as he was, there still was a certain amount of fear as death was imminent." I'm paraphrasing the exact words, but the meaning is accurate. After all, a dying person is about to go into an unknown world.

When any of us move a great distance away from loved ones and may never see them again, we feel a great fear and terrible sense of loneliness. The near prospect of dying is no different. Those who have developed a longing to be with God are inclined to be more at peace and even approach the last moments with relative joy, but leaving loved ones and entering into another world are even more final than making a move to another address far away. Jesus did give us important hints to prepare us for that important moment of our life and to understand God's attitude toward us as we are about to meet Him. Jesus did not want us to be afraid of that moment, but to approach it with peace by telling us the wonderful surprises His Father has in store for those who love Him. Those hints are most important in calming our souls and preparing us for that beautiful moment when we will see God face to face and experience His loving embrace and warm welcome.

In talking about our meeting with God, Jesus spoke some very consoling words. Even before describing the judgment, he mentioned at the house of Simon the Pharisee that the sinful woman's many sins were forgiven because, even though she was a sinner, God also saw loving goodness in her life. Our sensitivity to the pain and suffering of others around us and our care in reaching out to help those in need seem to be the key to relieving us of excessive fear as we approach God. It is interesting that in the only example Jesus gives of the Last Judgment, he does not mention our sins. He says:

> "Come, blessed of my Father into the kingdom prepared for you from the beginning of time. When I was hungry, you gave me food. When I was thirsty, you gave me drink. When I was naked, you clothed me. When I was ill, you cared for me. When I was in prison, you came to visit me."
>
> "When, Lord, did we ever see you in such straits?"
>
> And the Judge will answer, "As long as you did it to the least of my brothers and sisters, you did it for me."

Note that Jesus does not mention the commandments or the breaking of the commandments when describing the judgment. What Jesus seems to be saying quite forcefully is that God is willing to overlook our weaknesses and our sins if we have been struggling as best we can to overcome them; the proof of our struggling is how we treat God and people in need. In caring for others, we are attempting to observe Jesus' commandments to love and care for others. Merely avoiding evil is not the key. The Pharisees did that well. Even though they may have kept commandments that tell us what not to do, they were often insensitive to the suffering of others and to the pain they had inflicted on their fellow human beings by their ruthless laying of heavy burdens on people's lives. Jesus realized that commandments tell us what *not* to do. So, if someone only keeps the commandments, that person can go through his or her whole life and theoretically not do one good thing for another human being. That is what concerned

Jesus. But in Jesus' praising those who feed the hungry and the thirsty and care for others in need, He was recognizing that they were working on keeping the commandments by showing love and concern for God's suffering children. In speaking the way He did, Jesus gave us reason for great comfort as we approach our last days, if we have been caring and sensitive to the pain and suffering of others.

One of the most comforting experiences I had that allayed many of my own fears about dying was when a priest shared a dream he had with me. This priest was not a person who had devoted his whole life to charitable works, as Mother Teresa had. He was a gentle, uncomplicated man with ordinary simple goodness and sensitivity to others. A short time before he died, he had a dream; actually it seems to have been more a personal revelation from God. In this dream he was taken to a place more beautiful than anything he could have imagined, filled with beings more radiant and gorgeous than any human beauty he had ever seen. The places he saw in this dream were breathtaking. But he could not describe them because there was nothing in his whole life's experience that was as beautiful as what he saw in that dream.

All he could say was that he wanted with his whole heart and soul to be in that place. And he was told that he would be there in a short time. Two weeks later, filled with peace and longing, he died. He was only fifty years old and in relatively good health. Whether it was a dream or a vision God gave him to prepare him for his last days, we'll never know, but it was so much like what Saint Paul once said about heaven: "The eye has not seen, nor has the ear ever heard, nor has it ever entered the human imagination the wonderful things

God has prepared for those who love Him." That is what Jesus intended to hold out to all of us, peace and happiness for having tried to follow Him in our love and concern for God and for our hurting and suffering neighbors.

Another event had a profound effect on my understanding of how critical God is when we finally go to meet Him. Sister Dorothy Ederer, who was working with me at the time, and I were giving a retreat. A woman had shared with us her concerns about her husband, who was a good man and a good provider but very difficult to live with. He could be nasty at times. He was not a bad person but was very difficult. The woman told us that she was hoping her husband would come to the last talk I was giving on Sunday morning about heaven, as he had promised. All during my talk she kept looking around for him, but he never showed up. She was very disappointed.

In my talk I tried to describe heaven in ways that I knew from experience captivated people and in the end helped them to be not the slightest bit afraid to meet God; on the contrary, they wished they could go see Him right then. At the end I always told the people that not far from where we were, there was a spot where there were two special trees. If we walked between those two trees, we would immediately see God and He would warmly welcome us home to heaven. Then I would ask, "How many of you would like to come with me and see those trees and walk through them?" Always, practically everyone would put up his or her hand.

The woman who had been expecting her husband was very concerned about what might have happened to him. Sister Dorothy and I had to leave for another city, but when we arrived there we received a phone call from the lady. She and her friends had spent hours looking for her husband. They could not find him anywhere. Then they decided to walk way up along the beach. To their surprise, they found two trees, the only trees on the huge stretch of beach. Lying between the two trees was the body of the woman's husband. She knew God was trying to comfort her, her children, and all her friends, who were shocked at the coincidence.

These experiences and others similar have helped me greatly to grapple with my own fears and concerns about the last days. Our faith should bring us great comfort, as Jesus intended, so I share these experiences in the hope that they may be of comfort to my readers as well.

WHAT IS SIN?

*t*RYING TO UNDERSTAND SIN has been a very difficult problem for me. As children we were taught that there are mortal sins and venial sins. We were taught that mortal sins are serious offenses against God and destroy our relationship with Him. If we should die after committing one of those sins, we go to hell. The next worse evil is venial sin. It may be less serious than mortal sin, but it is still evil. These were horrible concepts to burn into children's minds, especially if the children were overly sensitive and impressionable. Yet they were realities that had to be dealt with. Offense against God is evil. Even as a child I had a tender love of God instilled in me. I never wanted to offend Him. But how can a child not do wrong things? Children can be difficult and at times nasty. Is God angry when we are like that as children? I thank God that confession was available for me as a child. What a healing sacrament it was for me. But when my struggles with faith were crushing me, I had to grapple with the idea of sin. What is it? What makes some things evil and other things not evil? How can people measure the wickedness of some sins so that they are deserving of eternal punishment and others are not, though we will still have to suffer for them? These were very difficult things to understand.

It took many years to adequately work with these concepts. Where to start was the biggest problem. What is God's attitude toward evil? What is His attitude toward sin? As I read the Old Testament, I could see how our concepts of sin originated and how the frightening attitudes toward sin developed. Punishment for sin was quick as lightning bolts. It made me wonder: Is God really like that, or is that the way people interpreted things that happened in nature or that just happened in the course of life? What is in God's mind? In the Torah, the first five books of the Hebrew Bible, God (Yahweh) is insistent on the promulgation of the most detailed moral laws and the severe punishment for violation of those laws. But in reading the gospels, I see a Jesus who is far different, who reflects a much more gentle attitude toward human weakness and human sin. Since Jesus said so frequently that He and the Father are one and when you know the Son you understand the Father, I was confronted with a serious problem. Jesus was more concerned about human suffering and the heavy burdens that people had to carry, and He spoke not about laws and commandments but about loving God and one another with a genuine love that feels a neighbor's pain or understands a neighbor's need. If Yahweh had the same attitude as Jesus, I could draw only two conclusions: Either who-

ever penned the Hebrew scriptures blamed what were ordinary natural catastrophes on Yahweh's anger over the people's
sinfulness and drew up the very severe laws and punishments
in the Old Testament, or God in the course of time changed
His attitudes and maybe His strategy.

Perhaps people in ancient days were more primitive and
had to be told how to treat one another and how to live in a
disciplined society. Perhaps severe punishments had to be leg-
islated to enforce order on the society. In Jesus' day the same
old law was still in force. Perhaps it was just God's strategy
that changed, more in keeping with Jesus' mission. But an interesting phenomenon appears when Jesus condemned those
who kept the laws to great perfection while having no love of
God or neighbor in the way they lived their lives and the way
they treated their fellow human beings. I feel sorry for the
scribes and Pharisees. They kept the law as well as any human
could. What troubled Jesus was the Pharisees' reputation for
their heartless, unforgiving attitude toward those who could
not keep the high ideals of the law and for their severe punishments of sinners other than themselves.

One example that comes to mind immediately is the story
of the woman caught in adultery. The Mosaic law said to
stone such people to death. Jesus warned the Pharisees who
dragged the woman before Him and a large crowd, "Let him
who is without sin among you cast the first stone." Only
when they realized, as one early Father of the Church relates,
that Jesus was about to reveal their personal secret sins when
writing in the sand did they drop their stones and slink away.
This shows another facet of God, or maybe what God was
really like until religious people began to interpret for others

what God was like: rigid, legalistic, punishing—attributes totally foreign to Jesus' gentle, understanding ways. "Come to
me, all you who labor and are heavily burdened, and I will refresh you. Take my yoke upon you and learn from me for I am
gentle and humble of heart and you will find rest for your
souls. My yoke is easy and my burden light"—this is the way
Jesus described Himself when inviting people not to be afraid
of Him. Such self-effacing tenderness in an all-powerful God!
It is hard to imagine Yahweh saying something like that in the
Old Testament.

What was Jesus' concept of sin? Is it the same as in the Old
Testament, but without the harsh punishments for the sinner?
Jesus tolerated a lot in people's lives. The apostles were certainly not paragons of virtue. They were coarse and crude, and
Peter cursed and swore even after being with Jesus for years.
James and John were vindictive, which shocked even Jesus.
Judas was a thief, yet Jesus entrusted him with holding
the money for the group. Even with the common people Jesus
seemed shockingly unconcerned about the spiritually un-
washed state of their lives. That had to be a big reason why the
crowds loved Him and followed Him around. He had the uncanny ability to accept them all where they were and never
pressured them to change radically. The people saw Jesus,
whom they knew was extraordinarily close to God, as a person who was not critical of their serious shortcomings. He expressed, in His manner and the look in His eyes and the way
He spoke to them, that He loved each one of them in a special way. There are people who have that special quality, but
Jesus had it in a way that reflected the unconditioned love of
God Himself. And that was a powerful attraction for the people to draw close to Him. They craved that kind of love and

acceptance, and it changed the lives of those who stuck with Him.

Jesus' apparent unconcern for sin was disarming until I realized that it was all part of His strategy. Sin offended Him. After all, He was God on earth living and moving among these crowds of sinners. But as I began to understand Jesus more deeply, His strategy became clear. He knew a person was a sinner before He even met the person. The story about Zacchaeus is a good example. Zacchaeus was chief tax collector in Jericho and had become rich. Jesus knew that. Why throw his sins up to him and humiliate the man? Jesus was too delicate and sensitive to treat ordinary people that way. What Jesus wanted was to win Zacchaeus over as a friend and a disciple. So, when He met the man, he invited Himself to the fellow's house for supper, surprising not only Zacchaeus but the admiring crowd. That nice gesture on Jesus' part won Zacchaeus' heart and changed his life. That was how Jesus drew people away from sin. He was a genius at what He did. He is perhaps the only reformer who fully realized that you cannot fight sin. Sin is a negative. It is merely the expression of an unfilled human need. What Jesus did was to offer something that could fill that horrible void in hurting people's lives, and in doing that He drew them within the healing embrace of God's love. And it worked.

Jesus' way of treating the apostles' shortcomings baffled me. Why did He put Judas in charge of the common purse of Jesus' apostles? Why was Peter still cursing and swearing after being with Jesus for three years? Why did He let them get away with their shocking behavior for so long? I found my answer to that question just a short time ago. To correct the apostles for their bad behavior and to pressure them to change their ways of acting or talking would change them only on the outside. Jesus was more concerned that their change should come from within, in a change of heart. That has to come naturally as the person grows spiritually. It cannot be forced. Jesus was willing to wait until the change came from within. It would then be an authentic change, flowing from a change of heart. This is why He never gave up trying to change their ways of thinking, their attitudes. He knew the change would come in time, as they grew.

In looking for the answer to Jesus' understanding of a sinner, I finally realized that a sinner was a thirsty person drinking polluted water or a hungry person eating poisoned food. Rather than just telling people they were drinking polluted water or eating poisoned meat, He offered them a spring of fresh, life-giving water to satisfy their thirst and real healthy food to fill their starving souls. People's empty souls must be filled with only what God can give. As Saint Augustine finally concluded after living a sinful life: "Our hearts were made for you, O God, and they will rest only when they rest in you."

In short, I have learned to define sin as any thought or action that contaminates our mind or damages ourselves or our neighbor, or intends to assault God, or wantonly damages His creation, to the detriment of humanity. So, God's concern over sin is not self-centered on His part. His concern is that in sinning, we damage ourselves or others. Even His attitude toward sin is expressive of His love and concern for us. What a strange God indeed! His thoughts and His ways are as high above our thoughts and our ways as the heavens are above the earth.

Even Jesus' warning about hell is not an expression of revenge on the part of God. Hell is a place where individuals choose to go because they want to have nothing to do with God. Heaven and hell are logical extensions of life on earth. If we live for God and for others, the moment after death nothing changes. We will still live for God and others, which is heaven. If we live only for ourselves and have totally and knowingly and willingly cut God and suffering human beings out of our lives, the moment after death that is not going to change. Hell is a logical extension of what our lives have always been, totally self-centered, and living with others who are totally centered around self. It is a place we choose. Interestingly, Jesus never said any human beings are in hell. He called hell a place for the devil and the angels who fell with him. We will never know whether any human beings have been so totally evil, and not just totally damaged and crippled, as to deserve a place like hell.

WHAT IS CHRISTIANITY?

*t*HE ANSWER TO THE QUESTION What is Christianity? was perhaps the biggest problem that haunted me for years because it was so difficult to identify. Since childhood, Christians, Catholics, Episcopalians, Methodists, Seventh-Day Adventists, Presbyterians, Baptists, and members of all denominations have been cradled in their parishes. We have all been brought up to love our parish church and the fact that we are members of the bigger family of our denomination. That denomination we call our Church. We were taught that it is our religion. What do we answer to the question "What religion do you belong to?"? We all name our religion, Catholic, Baptist, Episcopalian, Methodist. We have all been indoctrinated into our religion, its beliefs, customs, practices, unique identifying marks, spirit, and wonderful effects on the world, be it the local community or the world at large. We have grown up with a deep pride in our religion and try to interest others in this wonderful family to which we belong and all the goodness and fellowship we have found in it. When we have introduced a potential convert to our pastor so he or she can provide instructions for the new convert, what is taught in the instruction program?

The substance of the program is the teachings of the particular church or denomination. We as Catholics believe this, or we as Episcopalians believe this, or we as Presbyterians believe this. We continue session after session to go through the catalog of the doctrines and customs of the denomination. As part of the instructions we all mention that we are Christians, followers of Jesus Christ, who is our Lord and Savior, and who has redeemed us and won for us salvation. We talk about Jesus as the Son of God the Father, and as the Second Person of the Blessed Trinity, and that He is our way, our truth, our life, and the Holy Spirit also as God. If we follow Jesus' teachings during our lifetime, we will one day be taken to heaven to be with Him after our death. There we will be reunited with our loved ones. We also explain very carefully the particular theology that makes our denomination unique and different from all the other Christian denominations. When the new convert has been fully instructed in all the items of our faith, and gives assent to those beliefs, and is willing to make a faith commitment to Jesus Christ as Lord and Savior, we can then schedule the date for the baptism or reception into the religion. This approach is generally the same for all the denominations.

Does anyone have a problem with that approach? Clearly it makes sense and is very logical, and the end product is a person totally committed to the new religion and proud to be able to call him- or herself Catholic, Methodist, Episcopalian, or whichever.

Until recently I had never realized that that approach to religion, which has been so common for the past four hundred years, is fatally flawed. Why? For the very simple reason that it makes the institution the object of the person's commitment and loyalty, and makes every other Christian institution a dangerous and faith-threatening competitor. In many cases, the members of another denomination may not even be considered fellow Christians but, rather, possible threats to our faith and salvation. That approach instills in a person loyalty to doctrines and to an institution, and is the basis for so much hatred between religions in some countries. Religion should never be the cause of hatred between peoples. But, sadly, it is. What is disoriented about that approach? The answer is very simple. The institution of the Church is supposed to be the medium of the message, not the message. We have made the medium the message and have shifted people's faith to the medium and focused loyalty on it, the institution and its doctrines. Not that doctrines are wrong. True doctrines should reflect a deeper understanding of what Jesus taught or what logically flows from His message. They should reflect a more comprehensive understanding of Jesus and what intimately concerns Him. So, we cannot scoff at doctrines. But doctrines should not be so intimately tied in with the institution that they become merely part of a package of the theological beliefs of the institution, divorced from Jesus the Christ, which is what that archbishop demonstrated when he responded to a reporter by saying he was opposed to abortion because it was against the teachings of the Catholic Church.

The reason why that approach is so wrong is because the institution is not our religion. The institution is only a medium. Jesus is our religion, and Jesus Himself and what He teaches are the message. The message is important because it comes from Jesus, not because it is the expression of an institution's beliefs.

I do not mean to denigrate the Church. Although it is an institution, it is also the mystical body of Jesus. As such it is sacred and in a spiritual way organically bonded with Jesus. But we still have to draw the careful distinction that it is *not* Jesus. Jesus is God and is our Savior.

In the beginning of the spread of Jesus' message by the apostles, they did not teach doctrines as such, nor did they teach the New Testament. Carefully defined doctrines did not yet exist. The New Testament, in fact, had not yet been written. The apostles went out to all the world and talked to the people in this manner: "Let me tell you about my friend. His name is Jesus." Then they would continue telling their audience all about Jesus, who He was, what He was like, and what were the beautiful life-giving messages He came to bring to the whole world. It was all about Jesus. People accepted Jesus as their Lord and Savior, not the doctrines of a new religion. They fell in love with this Jesus whose life was so beautiful and reflected a God who loved them. If the apostles had presented a new theological system, the religion would never have taken hold. The flesh-and-blood Jesus the apostles presented as a loving, caring God promising life after death won the people's hearts.

The sad thing today is that there are very few people who can talk about Jesus with any depth, because there is no university or college that teaches about Jesus, in spite of all the angry denials when I say that. I would be happy to find a place that does teach a series of in-depth courses about Jesus, His life, His vision, His attitudes toward so many of life's situations. To date I have found none. I have been told often that the subject is not academic, so there is no place for Jesus in a college curriculum.

I have spent the last twenty-five years of my life going around the world talking about Jesus. The response has been electric. People of all denominations and of no denomination have come and sat for hours listening to stories about Jesus. It took me years of study and meditation to present these deep messages to people in a way that made Jesus real. It was not that I left out doctrines. The doctrines were woven into the fabric of Jesus' life and in His approach to people and His understanding of the complications in people's lives. The contrast between Jesus as the Good Shepherd and the theological rigidity of the scribes and Pharisees highlighted the beauty of Jesus' doctrine of forgiveness and acceptance of sinners where they were at a particular point in their lives. Things Jesus said and the way He treated people contained the seeds of many doctrines that flowed logically from His manifest attitudes portrayed in the gospels. In my talks I presented the doctrines as step-by-step organic growth emanating from the life and message of Jesus. The sacraments were not seven theological creations. The sacraments were deepening phases in Jesus' sharing of His divine life with us who have been baptized. Everything else in the talks pointed out that the organic development of Jesus' original message as the Holy Spirit, through the centuries, was deepening the Church's understanding of Jesus and His message.

I will never forget a story told to me by a priest who left the Church and married. His children are now in their thirties. Even though he resigned from the priesthood and was married in the Church, the man was always very involved in the work of his diocese. He called me one day to tell me of an experience he had just had with his archbishop. The former priest's son was very angry and disillusioned with the Church because of the way the local archbishop treated married priests in the archdiocese. However, the young man read *Joshua* one day, and it healed the terrible anger he felt against the Church and started him back to Mass, which pleased his father very much. The father told the archbishop how *Joshua* had helped the boy feel comfortable again with his faith. The father was shocked when the archbishop picked up a book and told the father, "This is the book he should be reading." It was a copy of the new Catechism of the Catholic Church.

That story epitomizes the sickness in our approach to people in desperate need of help. It is Jesus people crave. Jesus has within Him all that the human soul craves. People are trying desperately to find a flesh-and-blood Jesus, the Jesus the Jewish people saw walking down the streets of their villages, the Jesus who can fill their souls with the divine love. Their souls will rest only when they find the living Jesus as the companion of their souls, not when they find the Catechism, as beautifully written as it is for those who need clarification of their beliefs. When a person is suffering a terrible disease, you don't give him or her a pharmacology catalog filled with Greek and Latin names. You refer the person to a flesh-and-blood doctor who can heal. Jesus is our God. He is our religion. He is what we all crave in our pain-filled lives. He is our healer, not a catalog of doctrines. The Church is worried about Western Europeans having lost faith. It is not faith in God they have lost. It is faith in a Church hierarchy that preaches an institution in place of the living Jesus. If missionaries were trained in a deep knowledge of what Jesus was like as a person, and His love and care for the bruised and hurting sheep, the people of Western Europe would come back to the Church in droves because someone finally brought Jesus to them. I do not say this as theoretical possibility. I say it from experience. I say it after seeing the hundreds of thousands of people of all denominations who have come to my talks about Jesus and sat for hours to listen to a Jesus who heals their broken hearts and wounded souls. My heart has learned after many years to resonate with the pain in Jesus' heart when He pleaded, "I have come to set fire to the earth and what would I but that it be enkindled." He was so frustrated because nobody seemed to care. All the scribes and Pharisees cared about were their endless laws and traditions, which to them were more sacred than God or the desperate needs of the people's souls. Our hearts will rest only when we find God. We clergy are His ambassadors charged with bringing Him to life again in people's hearts. And if our seminaries do not teach about Him, where then will even the clergy get to know Him enough to be able to pass His love on to the people? No institution or catalog of its doctrines can be a substitute for the living Jesus.

28

WHAT IS THE GREATEST COMMANDMENT?

*W*HEN JESUS WAS ASKED what the greatest commandment was, his response was immediate. The first commandment is: "Love the Lord your God with your whole heart,
with your whole mind, with your whole soul and with all your
strength." The second is just like it: "Love your neighbor as
you love yourself. On these two is based the whole law and the
prophets." How wonderfully succinct! If that was how Jesus
evaluated the law, it indicates how much emphasis He placed
on love. Love and forgiveness were the message Jesus kept
preaching.

Since Jesus placed such emphasis on love as essential to our
relationship with God, it is incumbent that we as clergy manifest the same emphasis in our preaching His message to the
world of today. There is such need for love in our world,
where hatred and unforgiveness spread their poison through-

terflies. Not that we should not be concerned and disturbed about the desecration of our environment, because, God knows, we are going to destroy our world if we do not preserve God's gift to us, but it is appalling that righteous people can be so unconcerned about the plight of the most threatened species on earth, the human species. When have we ever seen a massive rally protesting the shameless treatment of the poor, and I don't mean the lazy poor, but the genuine poor, those who are struggling against great odds just to keep body and soul and family alive?

I have seen the poor victimized so often and so cruelly that I have cried many times from sheer frustration and almost despair over the degradation to which we have reduced the poor and helpless in our society.

So many of us seem to have lost the real message of Jesus, to reach out and care for those in need. I will never forget an incident that happened early one summer evening. I was driving down a busy street across from a shopping mall. It was raining, and as I drove I saw what I thought was a large bag lying in the street. As I approached I saw it was the body of a woman. I carefully drove the car to the curb and got out to see what had happened. The woman was alive but unable to move. I stood next to her and waved to oncoming cars, motioning for them to stop and help. People would slow down, take a curious look, and speed off. One after the other did the same. At least forty cars slowed down to look and then sped off. I could not believe people could be so unconcerned. It wasn't that I was a stranger. I was dressed in my clerical clothes with my Roman collar, and it was an open public place, so there was no reason why anyone should have felt it could be a threatening situation. Finally a man stopped and offered his help. He had someone call the police and an ambulance, and the lady was taken to a hospital. But I thought about that incident for weeks afterward wondering how people could be so unconcerned. They could see I was soaking wet from the rain and that there had to be something seriously wrong with the person lying in the wet street.

Jesus' kind of caring love is lacking in the hurting way we delineate sin and say that it is sinful if a person commits certain unlawful acts. That may be one way of defining sin, but that wording is cold and judgmental. A better description is that sin is damaging to ourselves, to others, or to the community or society at large. Jesus' meeting with the Samaritan woman at Jacob's well shows His delicacy toward a person who violated God's strict mandate on marriage. He had told the Pharisees who questioned him about divorce that a husband and wife become one flesh and that no one should violate that unity. It was a high ideal. Then he met the woman at the well and revealed that she had been married five times and that she was not married to the man she was living with. I am sure Jesus did not approve of the five weddings, but He acknowledged that there had been five marriages. The interesting thing about Jesus' comment is that He was not judgmental. Similar to the way he treated the prostitute in Simon the Pharisee's house, He also singled out the Samaritan woman for something special. He saw something good beneath the surface of her life and picked her to be the missionary to that village. It is also interesting that there is no record of Jesus telling the woman to leave the man she was living with. Could it be because He knew that having to leave would destroy her? Where would she go? Who would support her? Whatever the reasons, the message is very clear: Jesus could preach a high ideal of marriage, then show exquisite compassion to a person who fell far short of that ideal and see enough goodness beneath the surface of her life to pick her to be a missionary. Would we pick a person like that to be a reader in our churches or to be involved in any way in our parishes? Would Jesus?

Sometimes our way of presenting truth can be insensitive and hurtful to others. When the statement came out of the Vatican in 2004 that Christianity, and the Catholic Church in particular, is superior to other religions, many people around the world cringed. I suppose if we believe in our Church, we have to believe that way, since it expresses our choice in conscience that we have accepted what we believe to be the true message. But could it not be expressed with more delicacy?

For example, consider the impact of words like these: Before Jesus came, no founder of a religion taught about heaven. Heaven was not something offered by any other founder of a religion, no matter how high or noble his teachings and code of morality. Jesus revealed heaven as the place from whence He came, telling His followers that it was His home and the home of His Father. He promised that if people accepted Him and followed His way of life, they would one day go to heaven to live there forever with God and with all their loved ones. Only God could make that promise because it is His home, and only He could invite His followers to come and live there, this place that "the eye has not seen, nor the ear ever heard, nor has it ever entered into the human imagination what wonderful things God has prepared for those who love Him."

This gift of Jesus alone sets Christianity apart from every other religion, and the version of Christianity that has remained faithful to all of what Jesus taught since the earliest days of Christianity is also unique. I think phrasing the statement as I have done or in an even more polished way could say the same thing as the Vatican's statement, but would not appear arrogant. Instead, it would hold out something beautiful and positive to draw people to think about Christianity and the Church.

The delicacy of Jesus' love was expressed in so many beautiful ways in His approach to sinners and outcasts, it should inspire us to be more like Him in always preaching the highest ideals, but then showing sensitivity and compassion to those who fall far short of those ideals. He won sinners back into His Father's love by His understanding and compassion rather than by harsh criticism of their behavior.

If love of God and love of neighbor are the key to holiness and the essence of Jesus' moral teaching, should not the Church speak out more strongly and insistently on the many ways that Christian love is violated in human relationships and throughout society rather than concentrating so intensively on sexual morality? Sexual morality is most important in a world that is obsessed with sex, but sexual sins are not the only ones. What makes sexual sins so evil is that they are a sick abuse of human relationships and use others for selfish ends. Sexual sins have made a cheap social game out of a sacred gift from the Creator. Their evil flows from their lack of authentic love. That is what makes sexual sins evil. They are a gross violation of charity, or real love.

But there are other threats to our civilization and our humanity, and against God's creation. When do we speak out strongly against politicians' assassination of opponents' character, or cruelty and injustice in business relationships and destroying others in our attempt to get ahead, or the insidious ways the police try to entice panic-stricken suspects, sometimes innocent ones, into saying something that could be used to indict them on a totally unrelated issue, or promise immunity or a lesser sentence to someone to lie about a person the police would like to indict? Such acts may not be entrapment, but they are nonetheless disgustingly immoral and vicious, yet so common. When do we speak out against the criminal assaults against nature that threaten the very health and vitality of our planet? When do we speak out against the human sexual slavery so rampant today? When do we express our heartfelt concern about the geometric growth of the human population in undeveloped countries, when the capitalistic world has done woefully little to prevent the massive starvation and premature death of so many millions on earth today? Why do not the churches speak out loudly to prick the conscience of the world about these frightening crises? I would love to see papal encyclicals discussing these issues and the multifarious ways charity is trampled on in society rather than another encyclical on artificial birth control or priestly celibacy or statements opposing women priests or decrees limiting freedom of theological expression. Let theologians battle over theological ideas, as was done for centuries in the early days of Christianity, and let bishops and theologians clarify and debate issues rather than allow rules to be imposed from on high.

The Church's public discussion of pressing moral issues has

been sadly lacking, contrary to the priorities that were so critical in what Jesus defined as essential moral issues in the gospels. The Church must provide moral leadership not just in ecclesiastical matters, or narrow personal issues, but in issues that threaten the planet itself and the health and survival of vast numbers of indigent populations around the world. Electricity, water, food, medicine, education, freedom from human slavery—these are the universal needs of God's children. And the equitable distribution of the Father's heritage to all His children could well be the subject for the Church's message to the world.

29

FORGIVENESS

WHEN PETER ASKED JESUS how many times he should forgive, he was stunned by Jesus' answer: "seventy times seven times. As often as a person offends you." That is an issue that I had to struggle with for many years. It was difficult to make sense out of it. Jesus said that He came to lighten our burdens and to bring peace to our souls. This unlimited forgiveness seemed to be an impossible burden to have to carry through life. After many years it finally struck me that Jesus was not intending to place a burden on us but to give us a key to something very valuable. Nursing resentment for past injuries done to us by others prevents that wound from healing and causes it to fester. As time passes, the pain does not diminish; it intensifies. That festering sore of unforgiven injuries causes all kinds of unhealthy responses within our bodies as well as our emotions. The body chemistry generates dangerous compounds that course through us and cause a variety of illnesses. In fact, many people think that cancer is often caused by internally generated toxins formed from long-held hatred and resentment over past injuries.

While pondering Jesus' response to Peter, I went through the gospels again to see His reaction to people's nastiness toward Him. I was surprised. I could not see where Jesus ever took offense at what people said or did to Him. It is remarkable. With the scribes and Pharisees it was different. As religious leaders they were intentionally blind to Jesus' goodness. But even when He was sharp in His responses to them, He was like a doctor performing needed surgery on a sick patient, always trying to teach and help them to see the light. And when they invited Him to their homes for dinner, He always went, even though they were not always gracious toward Him.

What Jesus was giving us in His response to Peter was the key to true inner peace. If you want to have peace of soul, learn to forgive. Jesus' secret was His ability to see into people's hearts. Seeing their anguish and pain helped Him to understand their nastiness. So He could pity them rather than become angry with them. That is what we have to do: try to understand the pain in people's lives (so many people are crippled and damaged from childhood) and not take personally what they do to us. In this way we can avoid becoming angry and instead feel sorry for the misery that gnaws at their hearts. This is not easy, and becoming proficient at it is a lifetime job. However, in time we are able to forgive, and soon we begin to experience the freedom and the peace that flow from such an attitude. The pain and misery of other people's problems do not get stuck inside us like a fishhook. We don't take on their pain, and we find ourselves staying free and at peace. That was Jesus' intention when He responded to Peter as He did. After all these years of trying to understand it, it finally makes sense to me.

I recently read a story about a woman whose son was murdered. In the beginning she had hateful feelings toward the young man who killed her son, but that brought her no peace. She decided to go to the prison and meet the young man. He expressed his own sorrow to her for the terrible thing he had done. She told him that, as brokenhearted as she was, she forgave him. In time the two became friends, good friends. Her forgiveness and friendship did much to heal the young man of his own demons and drew him closer to God. The woman herself has since finally found peace. The beautiful relationship is healing both of them.

The story poignantly illustrates the beauty of Jesus' wisdom about forgiveness. It is the one virtue that more than anything else reflects the divine in a soul that clings to Jesus, and shows how beautifully a forgiving spirit can transform the human into the divine.

EPILOGUE

i have tried in the pages of this book to carefully retrace the steps in my faith journey, spanning over sixty years. It has been a painful yet joyful journey, and a most productive one. I have attained not only a deeper understanding of God and the critical role of Jesus in our destiny, but many rewarding insights into our journey through this life. I have learned that the word "sinner" is a name we call people. I have met individuals whom righteous people refer to as sinners; in my own experience with them, I have seen such a depth of goodness and compassion for others that to me they seemed more genuinely saintly than those who branded them as sinners. They would have been the ones whom Jesus would have befriended if He was here today. They were the type of people Jesus enjoyed spending time with. I also learned that I was never alone, that there was Someone always very close by and, indeed, within me, giving me strength in times of weakness and desolation, light in times of darkness, joy in times of great sorrow and pain, and the will to struggle on when continuing seemed futile. All along the way, I was given the strength, which I knew I did not have on my own, to take that next step into the unknown, in spite of my fears and my depression and my horrible anxieties, which tried to hold me back. Fortunately, that journey is a once-in-a-lifetime experience. I cannot imagine traveling that road ever again. I share it with you all in the hope it may be of some help in your own personal struggle to understand life's journey toward God and in trying to develop a relationship with God. If you do not become discouraged, it will become the most rewarding experience and adventure of your life.

Now after all these years, and in the twilight of my journey, I finally feel at peace with my Church. Even though I am still often disappointed with many of its rules and outdated customs, which are of human origin, and with the pain it causes to so many hurting souls, and with its exasperating resistance to rapid changes—sometimes changes that are so necessary—and also with the frightfully human elements in the Church, it is still, as Jesus said, the "pearl of great price" and the "treasure hidden in a field" that we should be willing to sacrifice all we have to possess. In my painfully exhaustive search I have also found that the Church has been adamant in its fidelity to the message of the gospels and the teachings of Jesus. Its insistence that only scripture and the beliefs of the earliest Christians taught by the apostles and recorded by the Fathers of the Church form the basis for theological tradition and are the only true sources for understanding the fullness of Jesus' teachings was important in my search for the integrity of Jesus' message. I developed a great admiration for the Church's insistence on the original sources, scripture, and authentic tradition as the only way of determining Christian truths. Its resistance to the changing fashions in morals so rampant in society and insistence that only the original sources can be used to ascertain Christian truth helped me considerably. While this approach made the Church look arrogant and insensitive to the demands of society because it would not put issues up to a democratic vote, I realized that Jesus' teachings could never be determined by what people wanted but only by what the original Christian sources have taught since apostolic times, by logical deductions from those sources, or by what those sources contained in seed form. Convinced that the Church has been faithful to the authentic teachings of Jesus for the past two thousand years, I finally felt comfortable and at peace in my commitment to my faith.

Looking back, I can now see that my whole life and many of its most important events, especially the most painful ones, were necessary for God to use me as a messenger of His love to others. Only in my later years did I realize that the experiences in my life were important because, without them, I could never have acquired what I needed to understand how God works in our lives. This became evident when I began to write the Joshua books. So many people told me that the series healed wounds they had suffered and lifted burdens they have carried all their lives. Only then, after so many personal testimonies, did I realize that God had been preparing me, as He prepares each of us, for a special job that had to be done. I hope that work is not yet finished and that there are still other ways I can make Jesus better known and loved by others and that, in finding Him, they may find the peace that only He can give.

About the Author

JOSEPH F. GIRZONE retired from the active priesthood in 1981 and embarked on a successful second career as a writer and international speaker. He is the author of several bestselling books, including *Joshua*, *A Portrait of Jesus*, and *Never Alone*. He lives in Albany, New York.